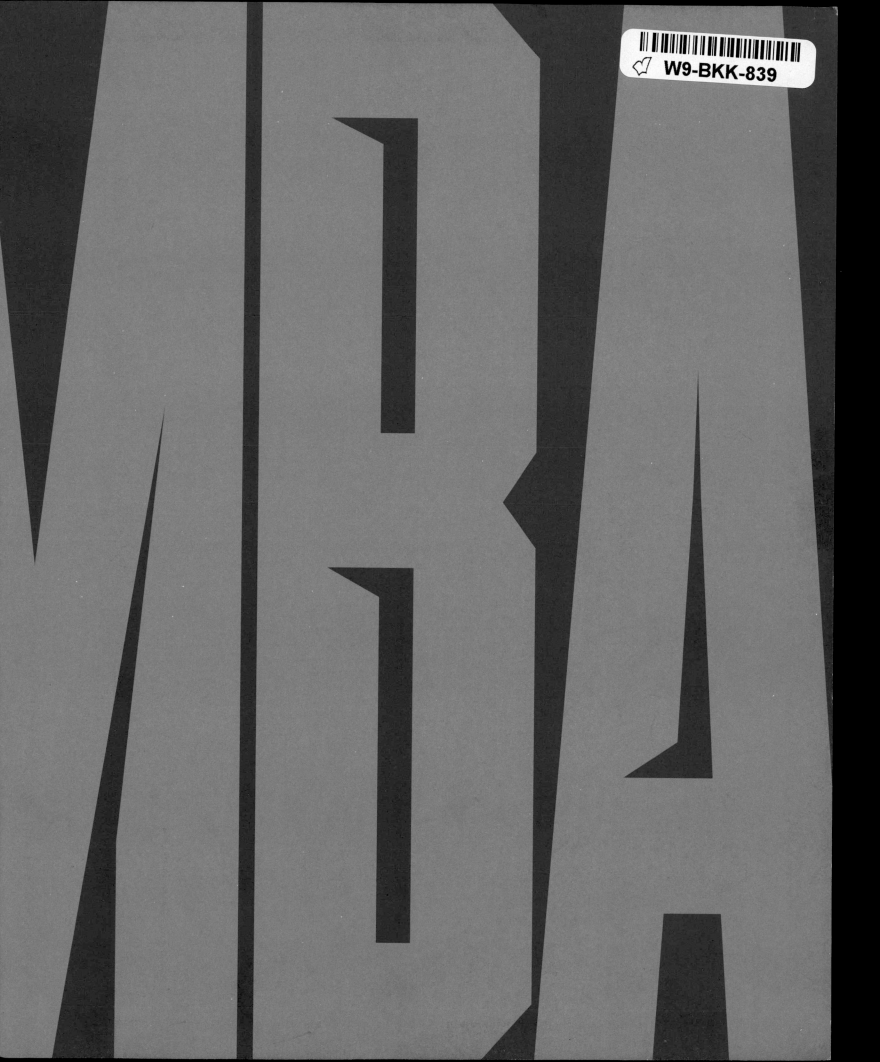

THE MAMBA MENTALITY

HOW I PLAY

Foreword by **PAU GASOL**

Introduction by **PHIL JACKSON**

Photographs and Afterword by **ANDREW D. BERNSTEIN**

MCD

FARRAR, STRAUS AND GIROUX
NEW YORK

MELCHER
MEDIA

I remember when, as a kid, I got my first real basketball.

I loved the feel of it in my hands. I was so enamored with the ball that I didn't actually want to bounce it or use it, because I didn't want to ruin the pebbled leather grains or the perfect grooves. I didn't want to ruin the feel.

I loved the sound of it, too. The tap, tap, tap of when a ball bounces on the hardwood. The crispness and clarity. The predictability. The sound of life and light.

Those are some of the elements that I loved about the ball, about the game. They were at the core and root of my process and craft. They were the reasons I went through all that I went through, put in all that I put in, dug as deep as I dug.

It all came back to that special tap, tap, tap that I first grew infatuated with as a boy,

This book is dedicated to the next generation of great athletes.
May you find the power in understanding the journey of others to help create your own.

Just make it better than this one.

—KB

To my family, thanks for your love, support, and patience.

—ADB

ACKNOWLEDGMENTS

My story, my career, my dedication would not exist without my wife, Vanessa. Thank you for your partnership, patience, and equally competitive spirit. You are my ultimate teammate.

Natalia, Gianna, and Bianka, I hope you find the inspiration in this book to go build your own Mentality. Each of you, above all else, is my pride and joy.

Thank you to the Hall of Fame photographer Andy Bernstein, who through the years perfected a craftsmanship with his lens that is unparalleled in the industry. One photographer, one athlete, one team, 20 years—without your work, this story could not fully come to life.

Tzvi Twersky, who spent countless hours helping me craft the perfect words to express and define the Mamba Mentality. Thank you for helping teach the next generation about the process and the craft.

Pau and Phil, you each challenged me to be the best version of myself. I hope your words help teach future athletes how to be the best version of themselves—in whatever they dream.

And special thanks to Rob Pelinka at the Los Angeles Lakers; Jay Mandel and Josh Pyatt at WME; Charles Melcher and Chris Steighner at Melcher Media; Darin Frank at Sloane, Offer, Weber and Dern, LLP; and the Kobe Inc. team, Molly Carter, Rita Costea, Matt Matkov, and Jay Wadkins.

—KB

Thanks to Kobe for the trust and joy of documenting 20 amazing years. Thanks to Joe Amati and David Denenberg of NBA Photos, Carmin Romanelli of Getty Images, Kelly Ryan, and Gail Buckland.

—ADB

Page 1: NBA All-Star Slam Dunk Contest, February 8, 1997, Cleveland

Pages 2–3: GOLDEN STATE WARRIORS, October 7, 2001, Away

Pages 4–5: MIAMI HEAT, January 17, 2013

Page 9: Practice, 1996, Hawaii

Page 11: Practice, 1996, Los Angeles

MCD

Farrar, Straus and Giroux

175 Varick Street, New York 10014

Printed in China

First edition, 2018

Library of Congress Control Number: 2018947512

ISBN: 978-0-374-20123-4

Our books may be purchased in bulk for promotional, educational, or
business use. Please contact your local bookseller or the Macmillan
Corporate and Premium Sales Department at 1-800-221-7945, extension
5442, or by e-mail at MacmillanSpecialMarkets@macmillan.com.

www.mcdbooks.com

www.twitter.com/mcdbooks • www.facebook.com/mcdbooks

10 9 8 7 6 5 4 3 2 1

Produced by Melcher Media

124 West 13th Street

New York, NY 10011

www.melcher.com

Founder and CEO: Charles Melcher

President and CRO: Julia Hawkins

Vice President and COO: Bonnie Eldon

Executive Editor/Producer: Lauren Nathan

Production Director: Susan Lynch

Senior Editor: Christopher Steighner

Contributing Editorial: Jeremy Woo

Cover and Interior Design by Nick Steinhardt, Smog Design, Inc.

CONTENTS

IN FEBRUARY OF 2008, MY LIFE CHANGED.

It was a pivotal moment in my career as a basketball player, but also in my life away from the sport. My path aligned with one of the greatest players to have ever played the game I love.

Just a few hours after being told that I'd been traded from the Memphis Grizzlies to the Los Angeles Lakers, I was on a cross-country flight to L.A., as opposite a city as you can find. The next morning, I had to go through a mandatory physical in order to finalize my trade. The Lakers were on the road and I couldn't wait to join my new teammates, so as soon as my physical was over I got on another plane to Washington, D.C. Kobe called me that morning, asking me to meet up once I arrived at the Ritz Carlton. It was past 1 AM when I finally got to my room, and shortly after I heard someone knocking at my door. It was Kobe. To me, that was a tremendous demonstration of a true leader, and our meeting had a huge impact on me, instantly. The message was clear: there was no time to waste, the moment was now, let's go get ourselves a ring. His mindset was unmistakable—it was all about winning.

One of the qualities that has made Kobe so successful, and always will, is his attention to detail. He always used to tell us: if you want to be a better player, you have to prepare, prepare, and prepare some more. His dissection of the game was at another level. I'm a player who watches a lot of tape, I like to watch my opponents' latest game to see how they are playing at the point that I'm about to face them, but Kobe took it a few steps further than that. I remember it like it was yesterday: we were in Boston during the 2010 Finals and I got a text from him. He wanted me to come to his room to show me a few clips of how the Celtics were covering the pick-and-roll and how we should attack it for the next game. I know for a fact that degree of detail, both in preparation and study, was a key factor in us winning those championships and many of the successes that Kobe achieved individually.

In my entire career, I've never seen a player as dedicated to being the best. His determination is unparalleled. He unquestionably worked harder than anyone else I have ever played with. Kobe knew that to be the best you need a different approach from everyone else. I remember a time when we got together as a team to have our annual dinner right before the playoffs. I was sitting next to him, and as we were getting ready to leave, he told me he was going to the gym to get a workout in. As much as I was very aware of the amount of extra time he put in outside of our regular work hours, it always shocked me how disciplined he could be even during a relaxed situation. When everyone else was thinking it was time for bed, his mind was telling him it's time to get ahead of the competition.

Over the years, a lot of people have wondered how difficult it must've been to play with Kobe. It really wasn't. All you had to do was understand where he was coming from, what he was about, and how badly he wanted to win. He would challenge players and coaches to match his intensity, his desire, to bring their very best every single day, not just at games, but at practices, too. Kobe wanted to find out what you were made of, and if he could count on you to help him win, plain and simple. I will always be thankful to him. He brought the best out of me as a basketball player, and he made me a stronger person, too. Our time was truly invaluable.

I'm the oldest sibling in my family and I always try to be an example for my two younger brothers, challenge them when I think they need to be and praise them when they deserve it. Kobe is the closest thing to an older brother for me. He never hesitated to tell me things as they were, never sugarcoated anything for me, and challenged me along the way so I could give my best at all times. Through the best moments, but especially during the harder ones, our bond only got stronger and we have always had each other's backs, just as brothers would.

Enjoy this magnificent book, which reflects some of what I've shared here with you, the qualities of an extraordinary person. I have no doubt that you will be inspired.

—**PAU GASOL**, teammate 2008–2014

WARNING: IF YOU ARE GOING TO INVEST YOUR TIME IN READING THIS BOOK, BE PREPARED FOR AN ADVENTURE IN HIGH-LEVEL BASKETBALL.

It will certainly offer a deeper understanding of the detailed and dedicated way Kobe Bryant approached the game. It's one thing to have talent, but another to have the drive to learn the nuances. James Naismith is credited with having said "basketball is an easy game to play, but a difficult game to master." This is a window into the mind of someone who mastered it. The combination of Andy Bernstein's exceptional photography and Kobe's insights might make you a better player if you're inclined.

Kobe came into the NBA with a desire and talent to become one of the greatest players of all time. He achieved that goal through his dedication and perseverance. The opportunity to play for the Lakers, a historic franchise, gave him an audience and a forum, but his level of success came entirely from within.

Kobe and I first met in 1999 at the Beverly Hills Hilton, on the day I was formally announced as the Lakers' coach. We were in a suite, before I went down to meet members of the press assembled in the ballroom. Kobe wanted to impress upon me how happy he was to have the opportunity to play in the triangle system—and how much he already knew about it. He was already a "student of the game," and had studied various aspects of the offense. Here he was, 20 years old, sounding like he'd been a pro for a decade.

By nature, the triangle offense is confining and disciplined. There is little room for a player to just go rogue. It was a planned, programmed way to play. Push the ball upcourt and look for an early shot; if it's not there, build the triangle; read how the opponent's defense is going to react; attack their weakness and apply your strengths. My twin sons are just one year younger than Kobe, so at that point I had a pretty good perspective on young men and their varying ability to focus on tasks. I had also had the privilege of coaching a number of players who had said the same thing during my tenure with the Chicago Bulls. Even at that young age, though, Kobe kept true to his word about being a student of the game.

Kobe actually broke a bone in his wrist the very first game of preseason that year, and missed the first 14 games. We had gotten off to a good start without him, and I was concerned he might require some "break-in" time to fit into the mix. It wasn't a problem. He kept the team winning as his first priority and we kept rolling.

A month or so after he returned to active play, I received a call from Jerry West, who wanted to relay a conversation he'd had with Kobe. Kobe had called to ask him how he and Elgin Baylor had both been able to score 30-plus points a game while sharing the ball on the same team back in the 1960s. After Jerry probed a bit, Kobe admitted he was worried he wasn't going to score enough points to become "one of the greatest players in the NBA." This concerned me, because as a coach I didn't care how many points a player scored—only the final numbers on the scoreboard. But Kobe knew what he was capable of doing, and felt limited by our system. That clash had all the warning signs of becoming a problem. Of course, there was real substance behind his drive—he went on to total 33,643 points in his career, ahead of Michael Jordan and just behind Karl Malone and Kareem Abdul-Jabbar.

That first year, Kobe played alongside Ron Harper in a two-guard system at the top of the floor. They were in charge of "setting the table"—recognizing when the fast break was over, secondary action was limited, and it was time to set up the triangle system. Naturally, there was always a temptation to push the envelope, and sometimes Kobe would go rogue. He'd break from the plan to create an opportunity for himself, and it would jam up our offensive flow. So we had our conversations about not trying to take over a game. We also had our film sessions, centering on what skills made a guard a good playmaker. In retrospect, Kobe was as patient with me as I was with him. We tolerated each other, and the result was that he came to understand how disciplined our team had to become in order to win that coveted championship. As much as he loved to score, Kobe usually knew or intuited what the right thing to do for the team was in the moment.

The Lakers had been a bridesmaid the past two seasons, winning a ton of games but getting swept out of successive playoffs. Shouldering the pressure that came with that history, Kobe, of course, made the plays. The Lakers got over the stigma of coming up short and went on to win three championships in a row. Each of those years was dramatic and full of memorable games and moments. Kobe was the driving force, while Shaquille O'Neal, the Diesel, was the focal point of the offense—"Get the ball to the big fella," as we'd say. The group of Lakers went to four finals in five years, in essence creating a dynasty.

The next segment of Kobe's career was when his maturation took place. After the Shaq-Kobe era came to a close, he became the senior statesman for a team that had lost all of its other starters via retirement or trade. He was the major thrust of the team and its nominal leader, perhaps by default. And leadership is a tough thing to master, especially when you know a championship is beyond the reach of your personnel.

At one point in our early years with the Lakers, Kobe and I stood together before practice and watched five of the other players hold a shooting contest. It was similar to the game "Cat," where a player had to mirror and match the shooter before him, or he was eliminated. They had asked me to hold off the start of practice because the game went around the entire arc, using both corners, both wings, and the top. I asked Kobe, competitive as he was, why he didn't play against his teammates, and he said it was because he wasn't a three-point shooter. But in the year that followed, he was determined to fix that: During the off-season Kobe worked diligently on his three-point shot. It was always about the details. And in the 2005–06 season, Kobe went off and averaged more than 35 points a game, leading the NBA in scoring. He had become a scoring machine.

I could go on listing records and accounts of his scoring prowess, but that was really a side note to Kobe's evolution as a player. My staff would meet at 8:30 AM at our facility before a practice or game to prepare for the coming day. More often than not, by the time I pulled in, Kobe would already be parked in the car next to my designated spot, taking a nap. He would be in the gym well before that, maybe by 6 AM to get his pre-practice workout done before anyone else showed up. That was the trademark of the final 10 years of his career. Kobe led by example for his teammates. They couldn't keep up—but they were always challenged by the example he set.

In 2007, I met with Kobe to discuss the Olympics in China. That team was packed with stars and had practiced together that summer in preparation for the next year, when they would go on to win gold. My message to Kobe was this: If you are going to do the extra off-season things, you must recognize you only have a certain amount of time left on your legs. Practice is not a big concern of mine, you know the system. I will give you as much time as you need between games to recover if you will keep your leadership intact by being present. He would do his physical therapy while the team went through their skills and drills and come onto the court when competitive action commenced. He encouraged his team and sometimes played the coaching role for the second unit. I was watching Kobe go through extreme routines to get himself ready to play games and thought there might be a window of five or six years left in his career. Again he changed the landscape, and his determination to extend his physical prime blew out the norm. He played almost 10 more years of NBA high-intensity basketball, which stands as a measure of his character.

The photographs in this book are a testament to the manner in which Kobe has thought about the game. In fact, the way Kobe approaches basketball has prepared him for the "next" phase of his life, one that already looks as interesting and intense as his long career with the Lakers.

—**PHIL JACKSON**, coach 1999–2004, 2005–2011

WHEN IT CAME TO BASKETBALL, I HAD NO FEAR.

What I mean by that is: if I wanted to implement something new into my game, I'd see it and try incorporating it immediately. I wasn't scared of missing, looking bad, or being embarrassed. That's because I always kept the end result, the long game, in my mind. I always focused on the fact that I had to try something to get it, and once I got it, I'd have another tool in my arsenal. If the price was a lot of work and a few missed shots, I was OK with that.

As a kid, I would work tirelessly on adding elements to my game. I would see something I liked in person or on film, go practice it immediately, practice it more the next day, and then go out and use it. By the time I reached the league, I had a short learning curve. I could see something, download it, and have it down pat.

From the beginning, I wanted to be the best.

I had a constant craving, a yearning, to improve and be the best. I never needed any external forces to motivate me.

During my rookie year, at first, some scouting reports said I wasn't tough. The first time I went to the basket in games, I'd get hit and the defense would think they had me. I'd come back the very next play and pick up an offensive foul just to send them a message.

I didn't need that extra push to be great, though. From day one, I wanted to dominate. My mindset was: I'm going to figure you out. Whether it was AI, Tracy, Vince—or, if I were coming up today, LeBron, Russ, Steph—my goal was to figure you out. And to do that, to figure those puzzles out, I was willing to do way more than anyone else.

That was the fun part for me.

BY THE TIME I REACHED THE LEAGUE, I HAD A SHORT LEARNING CURVE.

I DID BIBLICAL WORKOUTS.

I started lifting weights at 17, when I got to the NBA. Nothing fancy, just basic, time-tested lifting methods that focused on strengthening one group of muscles at a time. Over the meat of my career, whether we were in season or it was summer, I would lift for 90 minutes on Monday, Tuesday, Thursday, and Friday. When I say lift, I mean heavy, hard, can't-feel-your-arms type of lift. After that, I would go into the gym and shoot.

Over the years, my routine might have changed some but my philosophy never did. If something has worked for other greats before you, and if something is working for you, why change it up and embrace some new fad? Stick with what works, even if it's unpopular.

MY MIDNIGHT WORKOUTS HAVE BECOME A THING OF LEGEND.

They were always purposeful. They were born from a mix of obsession and real-world responsibilities.

I always felt like if I started my day early, I could train more each day. If I started at 11, I'd get in a few hours, rest for four hours, and then get back to the gym around 5 to 7. But if I started at 5 AM and went until 7, I could go again from 11 until 2 and 6 until 8. By starting earlier, I set myself up for an extra workout each day. Over the course of a summer, that's a lot of extra hours in the gym.

At the same time, starting early helped me balance basketball and life. When my kids woke up in the morning I was there, and they wouldn't even know I had just finished at the gym. At night, I'd be able to put them to bed, then go work out again during my own time, not theirs.

I wasn't willing to sacrifice my game, but I also wasn't willing to sacrifice my family time. So I decided to sacrifice sleep, and that was that.

STARTING EARLY HELPED ME
BALANCE BAKETBALL AND LIFE.

FILM STUDY IS ALL ABOUT DETAIL.

From a young age—a very young age—I devoured film and watched everything I could get my hands on. It was always fun to me. Some people, after all, enjoy looking at a watch; others are happier figuring out how the watch works.

It was always fun to watch, study, and ask the most important question: Why?

The biggest element that changed over time, however, was I went from watching what was there to watching for what was missing and should have been there. I went from watching what happened to what could have and should have happened. Film study eventually became imagining alternatives, counters, options, in addition to the finite details of why some actions work and others don't work.

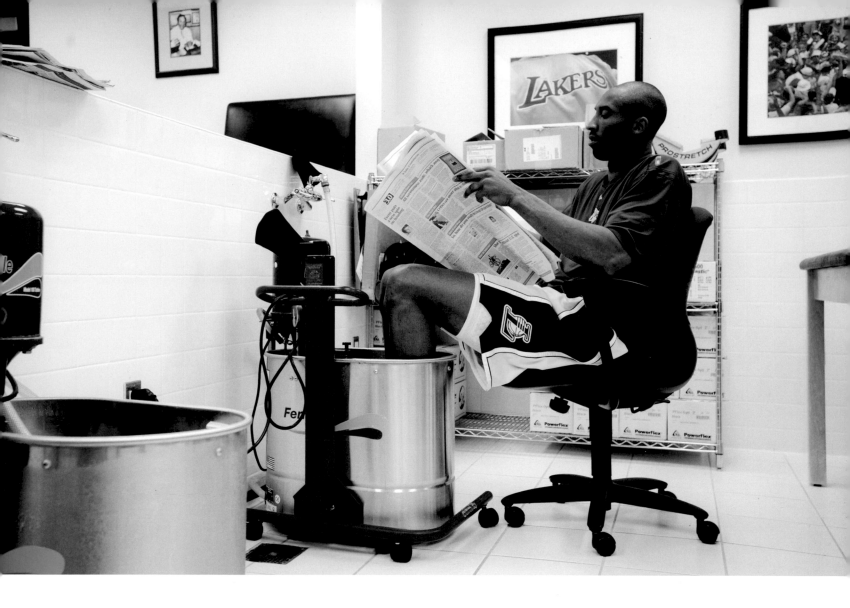

I DIDN'T TRAIN ONLY MY BODY— I TRAINED MY MIND, TOO.

The only way I was able to pick up details on the court, to be aware of the minutiae on the hardwood, was by training my mind to do that off the court and focusing on every detail in my daily life. By reading, by paying attention in class and in practice, by working, I strengthened my focus. By doing all of that, I strengthened my ability to be present and not have a wandering mind.

Just as important as reading was cultivating relationships with the greats who'd come before me. As evidence of this, look at my retirement ceremony and who was there. That will tell you how I managed to get my jerseys up there. You had Bill Russell, Kareem Abdul-Jabbar, Magic Johnson, Jerry West, James Worthy. Those guys taught me the lessons that gave me an edge over my competition. That's why I think it's so important to have those mentors, those north stars, who you learn from and look up to.

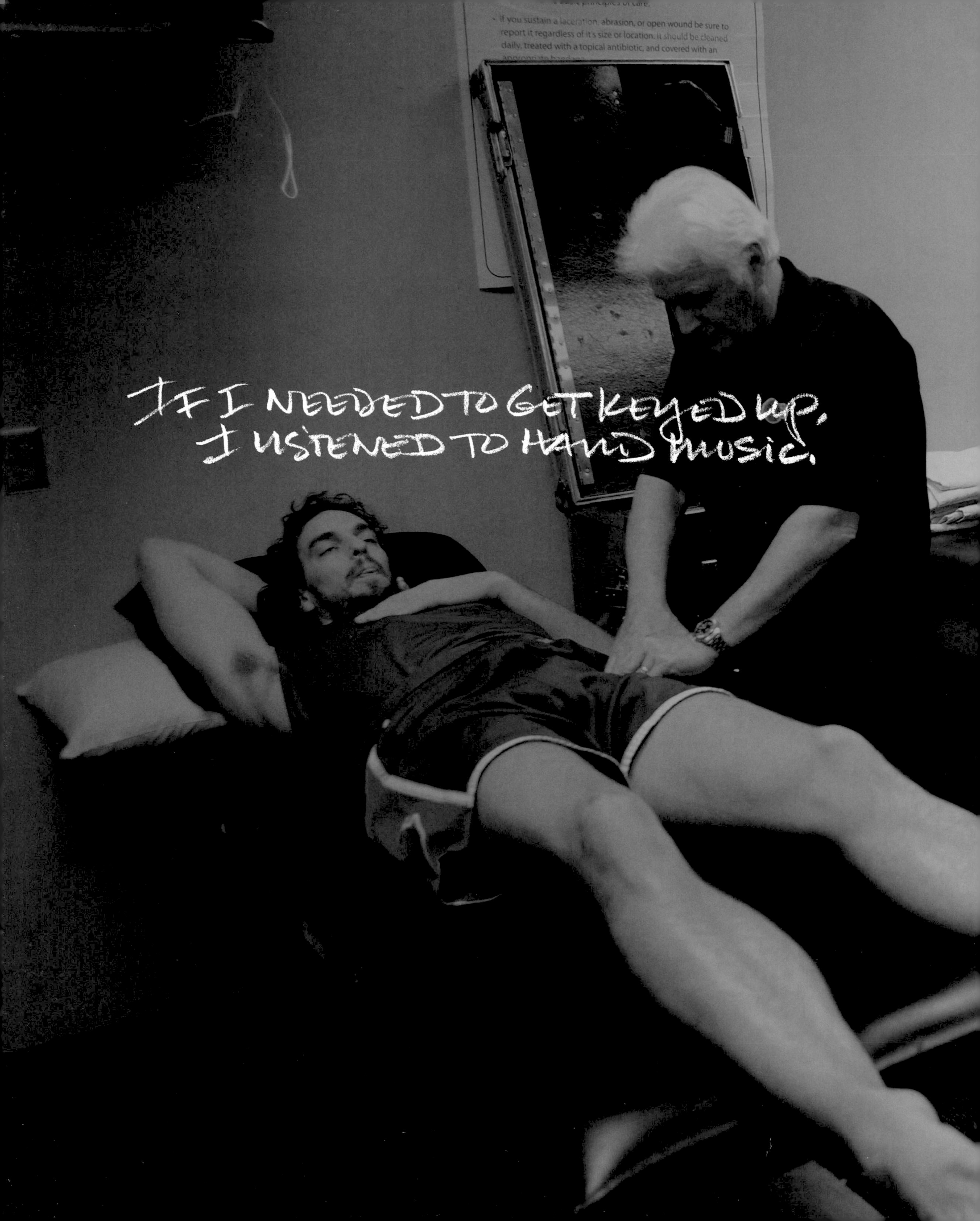

IF I NEEDED TO GET KEYED UP.
I LISTENED TO HARD MUSIC.

MY MENTAL PREPARATION VARIED BASED ON MY HEADSPACE.

It varied based on where I thought my head needed to be for that specific game. If I needed to get keyed up, for example, I listened to hard music. If I needed to soothe myself, I might play the same soundtrack I listened to on the bus in high school to put me back in that place.

It's all about putting me in the place I need to be in for that game. Some games required more intensity, so I would need to get my character and mind in an animated zone. Other games, I needed calm. In that situation, I wouldn't listen to music. Sometimes, even, I would sit in total silence.

The key, though, is being aware of how you're feeling and how you need to be feeling. It all starts with awareness.

YOU HAVE TO HAVE AN UNDERSTANDING
CIRCLE OF FAMILY AND FRIENDS.

If you really want to be great at something, you have to truly care about it. If you want to be great in a particular area, you have to obsess over it. A lot of people say they want to be great, but they're not willing to make the sacrifices necessary to achieve greatness. They have other concerns, whether important or not, and they spread themselves out. That's totally fine. After all, greatness is not for everybody.

What I'm saying is greatness isn't easy to achieve. It requires a lot of time, a lot of sacrifices. It requires a lot of tough choices. It requires your loved ones to sacrifice, too, so you have to have an understanding circle of family and friends. People don't always understand just how much effort from how many people goes into one person chasing a dream to be great.

There's a fine balance between obsessing about your craft and being there for your family. It's akin to walking a tightrope. Your legs are shaky and you're trying to find your center. Whenever you lean too far in one direction, you correct your course and end up overleaning in the other direction. So, you correct by leaning the other way again. That's the dance.

You can't achieve greatness by walking a straight line.

Respect to those who do achieve greatness, and respect to those who are chasing that elusive feeling.

I ALWAYS STARTED OFF MY ROUTINE CLOSE TO THE BASKET.

I would start off short and work on my touch. Always. Always. Always. Get my muscle memory firing. Then, I'd move back, work for a bit, move back again, and repeat the same process. After that, I'd start working on situational looks that I was going to get that night. I'd walk my body through the scouting report, and remind it of things it had done thousands and thousands of times before.

I never had a set routine, an ironclad formula that I practiced night after night. I listened to my body and let it inform my warmup, because there are always variables. If I felt the need to shoot extra jumpers, I'd shoot more. If I felt the need to meditate, I'd meditate. If I felt the need to stretch for a longer duration, I'd stretch. And if I felt the need to rest, I'd sleep. I always listened to my body. That's the best advice I can give: listen to your body, and warm up with purpose.

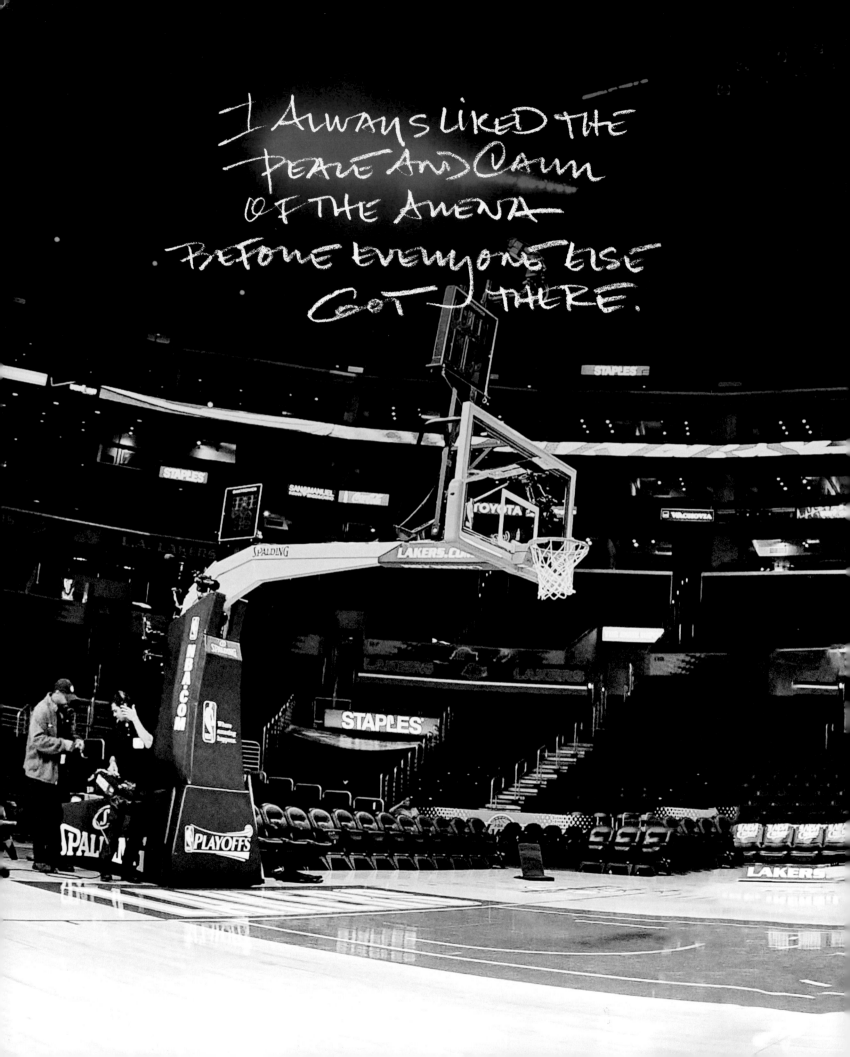

I ALWAYS LIKED THE PEACE AND CALM OF THE ARENA BEFORE EVERYONE ELSE GOT THERE.

It's just me and the basket, the court and my imagination, dreams. There's something about being in a big arena when no one else is there. It gives me a sense of nirvana and also prepares me for the game. When I jogged out of the tunnel and the fans were screaming and it's loud, the noise didn't impact me. Mentally, I was able to remember the stillness of the earlier moment and carry that with me.

I COULD RUN ALL DAY LONG.

If you want to be a great basketball player, you have to be in great shape. Everyone talks about the fancy workouts and training sessions, but I also worked relentlessly to make sure that my legs and lungs were always at peak performance.

My cardio workouts centered around recovery—that is, the time it takes to recover in between sprints. The reason I placed an acute focus on that element is because basketball dictates short bursts where you run as fast as you can, then have a moment to recover, then burst again. I wanted to make sure that I would always be ready for the next burst of action.

Specifically, I did a lot of timed work on the track where I would incrementally decrease the amount of time between each set until, after a full off-season, my recovery time would be almost nil.

I ASKED A TON OF QUESTIONS.

I was curious. I wanted to improve, learn, and fill my head with the history of the game. No matter who I was with—a coach, hall of famer, teammate—and no matter the situation—game, practice, vacation—I would fire away with question after question.

A lot of people appreciated my curiosity and passion. They appreciated that I wasn't just asking to ask, I was genuinely thirsty to hear their answers and glean new info. Some people, meanwhile, were less understanding and gracious. That was fine with me. My approach always was that I'd rather risk embarrassment now than be embarrassed later, when I've won zero titles.

JUST DO IT.

I never thought about my daily preparation. It wasn't a matter of whether it was an option or not. It was, if I want to play, this is what I have to do, so I'd just show up and do it.

My routine was grueling. It involved early mornings and late nights. It involved stretching, lifting, training, hooping, recovery, and film study. It involved putting in a lot of work and hours. It's—no lie—tiring. For that reason, a lot of players pare down their lifting and training during the season. They try conserving their energy. Not me, though. I found that, yes, this work might be strenuous on the day-to-day, but it left me stronger and more prepared during the dog days of the season and the playoffs.

Sometimes, as part of that, I'd be so tired I'd need a quick nap at some point during the day. Whether before practice or a Finals game, on the bus or trainer's table, five hours before tip or 60 minutes, if I was tired I would doze off. I always found that short 15-minute catnaps gave me all the energy I'd need for peak performance.

BREAKDOWN IS AS IMPORTANT AS SETUP.

While you're playing the game, there are no distractions. Right after the buzzer sounds, a lot of people shower and change as quickly as they can. For me, though, there was more work to be done.

Ice, the old reliable, was the status quo for me after every game, every practice. I'd always ice with two bags on the front and back of my knees and on my shoulder, and both feet in an ice bucket for 20 minutes. This would help bring down the inflammation and kick off my wind-down of this session and jumpstart my gear-up for the next.

BATH TIME

Certain days, my whole lower body felt stiff. On those occasions, when my body was seemingly locked up from the waist down, I would use the full body tub to mimic the contrast therapy I always underwent on my ankles (see opposite). Again, it's important to listen to your body and let it dictate your daily prep. Bath time had a bonus benefit: I'd use the quiet break to catch up on reading, always studying to improve my game.

A SONG OF ICE AND FIRE

Contrast therapy has been around forever, but I was put on to it back in high school. After that, I was religious about partaking in it before every game to either help loosen up my joints, or numb certain body parts. Over time, I developed a very particular routine. I would start with four minutes of cold—I mean *cold*—water and switch to three minutes of hot. Then, I would go with three minutes of cold, two minutes of hot. The sequence would continue, two cold, one hot, before ending with one minute in the cold water. This was only one small part of my process to prepare for battle.

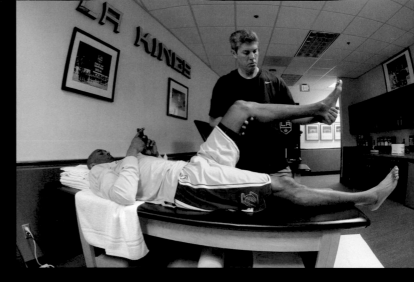

CAUSE AND EFFECT

Pain in one area of your body often stems from an imbalance somewhere else. With that in mind, it's important to treat the root cause and not the effect.

I always made sure my ankles were activated and moving. If your ankles are stiff, that can create problems in the knees, hips, back, and all the way up. So, I'd spend a lot of time before games working on my ankles—the core of the problem—so that I wouldn't exacerbate the symptoms.

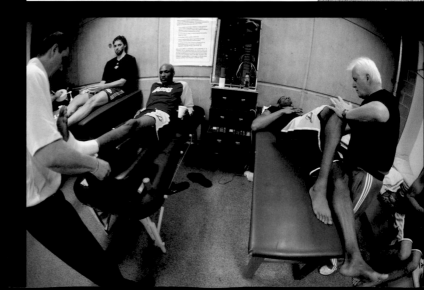

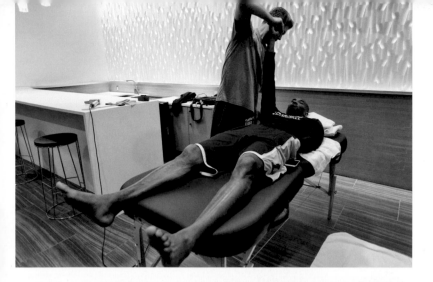

CALIBRATING THE CANNON

I would begin stretching a couple of hours before games. Then, as the game got closer and closer, I would start doing more active, more range-of-motion things to get ready. This, in particular, was a big part of getting prepared and activated during my last year. We would make sure my shoulder was sitting back correctly and it wasn't rotating forward.

I WASN'T ALWAYS OLD.

As a kid, I didn't have to do all of the stretching and warming up. I would go out, get my shots up, put in work, and then I'd have some time to myself. Sometimes, I would even just chill and watch some TV. I could have gotten up, right there and then, and windmilled. As I aged, I was meticulous about listening to my body and adjusting accordingly.

MY HANDS STILL HURT.

My broken finger would get tight. A torn tendon in my pinky finger never recovered. Due to all that, I would try to warm my hands up and do hand-strengthening exercises. Before games I would get an oversized ball and stretch my hands around and squeeze it, just to wake up the tendons and muscles in my hand. My finger, in particular, is still inflexible to this day. But I never let these impediments stop me.

MY ROUTINE CHANGED OVER TIME; MY APPROACH DIDN'T.

I always tried to train and prepare intelligently, but as I got older my pre- and post-game routine evolved. When you're younger, you work on explosive things and as you get older your focus shifts to preventive measures. That's all par for the course. The only aspect that can't change, though, is that obsession. You have to enter every activity, every single time, with a want and need to do it to the best of your ability.

WE ALL GOT READY FOR GAMES DIFFERENTLY.

When Shaq and I played together, generally, we'd get
taped at the same time. That would give us an opportunity
to joke and goof around or to talk crap. For Shaq and me,
as anchors of the team, this would help get us up and ready
for the game.

More than that, this would set the tone for the team. The
energy of the club is all sitting right there. This was our
moment to smile and laugh. As the game drew closer, we
got serious. That dichotomy, that changing of airs, was
important for our teammates to see and understand.

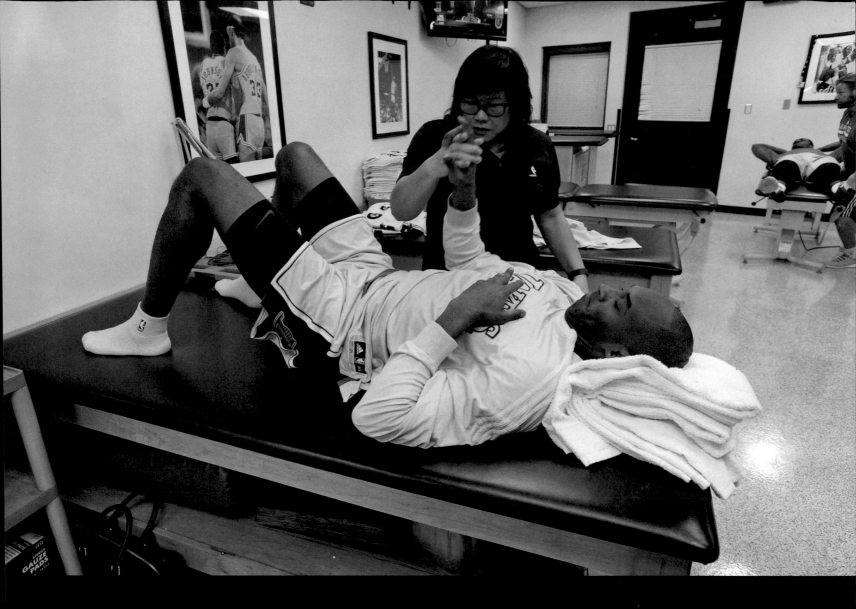

JUDY SETO HAS BEEN WITH ME FOREVER.

When I was a rookie, Judy Seto was a young up-and-comer. One time, after I tweaked an ankle, she was assigned to me. It immediately became apparent to me that she was as obsessive about training as I was about basketball, and we formed an immediate and unbreakable bond. Over the years, we both continued to learn and grow in our individual crafts. In doing so, we were able to push each other to be our best.

It's safe to say I would not have been able to play as well or as long without her as my physical therapist. She helped me recover from every single surgery I ever had, and she was always there for me. Literally. Whether it was a family

GARY VITTI WAS CRUCIAL TO MY CAREER.

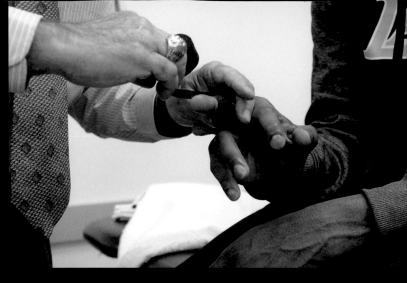

First of all, Gary was an Italian craftsman with tape. He just made art out of tape jobs. You can tell when people love what they do, and he loved his craft. No matter where the tape was going—finger, ankle—he made it look beautiful. If the tape had bubbles or bumps, Gary would unwrap it and start again. Everything had to be smooth, had to be perfect. He was a master, and I gave him a lot of opportunities to practice.

He's not the only trainer who was vital to my well-being. Judy Seto (see previous page) was critical, as was my neuromuscular therapist, Barrence Baytos. I had a great team of people around me.

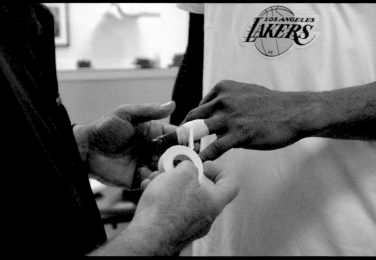

They were obsessive about their own crafts, which made it easy for me to trust them. Once I trusted them, I listened to my body, and it told me they were doing good work. I felt better, stronger, and more prepared when I worked with them.

MASTER OF THE MIX-TAPE

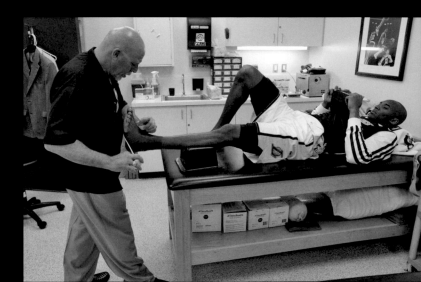

Over the course of my career, Gary and I alternated the tape jobs on my ankles. The decision was dependent on where, physically, my ankles were that year. Some years, the focus was on stability, so I'd use all white tape. Other times, when my ankles felt stable and solid on their own, I'd use a more elastic tape, which allowed for more spring and movement. One of the most important aspects of the game is listening to your body, and preparing it accordingly. I always kept that in mind.

I HURT MY ANKLE. BADLY.

This was Game 2 of the 2000 NBA Finals—the worst sprained ankle of my career. From there, it was on me to figure out a way to play and be tactical. I knew what I could and couldn't do, which directions I could push off and how much force I could apply. After establishing that, it was just a matter of altering my game within those constraints to continue dominating.

To do that, despite the injury, I had to maintain control and dictate where I was going to go with the ball and how I was going to play. I had to, even on one ankle, keep the advantage in my court and never let the defense force me to do something I didn't want to do. That was the key here, and that's the key always.

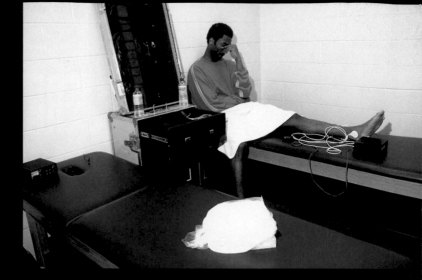

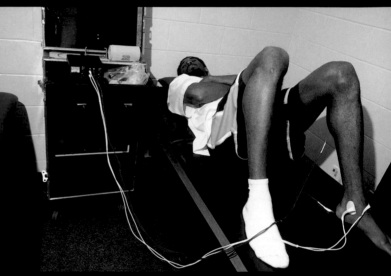

NBA 2K

After that injury (see opposite), I missed Game 3 but managed, thanks to stimulation therapy, to play the rest of the series. This treatment involves wires that deliver low-level electrical current directly through your skin. It actually helps bring the pain down. But the ankle was so bad that, to be honest, I couldn't hoop much that summer. What I did do, though, was take up tap dancing.

That's right: tap dancing.

That was my worst sprain, but it certainly wasn't my first. I realized at that point I needed to be proactive about strengthening my ankles. After researching the matter, it became apparent that tap dancing was going to be the best way to build up my ankle strength while simultaneously improving my foot speed and rhythm. So I hired an instructor and started going to the studio. I worked on it all of that summer and benefited for the rest of my career.

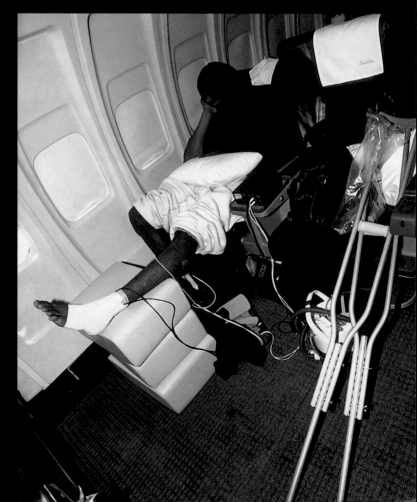

JERRY WEST

Jerry West and I had a father-son type of relationship

He was there for a lot of the early, big moments in my career. I specifically remember riding with Jerry in a Lexus to my first workout. At the time, I was thinking, "Wow, I'm sitting next to *the* Jerry West." I asked him a ton of questions about moments and games in his career. Honestly, I don't know whether he was intrigued or annoyed, but he answered them all.

I learned shortly thereafter that Jerry is one of those guys who shoots it straight with people he respects. If he really cares about you, he's going to tell you things that you don't want to hear. And he always shot it straight with me.

It's been a beautiful relationship.

MAGIC JOHNSON

I MET MAGIC DURING MY FIRST YEAR IN L.A.

We met at UCLA during a day of pickup runs. I was there stretching, getting ready to play, and he walked in. That was my first time—and I think last time—playing with Magic. That was pretty sweet. More than that, it was good to talk with him. I revere the players who made the game what it is, and cherish the chances I had to pick their brains. Anything that I was seeing or going to see, any type of defense or offense or player or team—they had already encountered years before. I talked with them to learn how to deal with those challenges. After all, why reinvent the wheel when you can just talk to the wheels that were created before? Magic Johnson was a special player, and I learned a lot of especially important lessons from his game.

Namely, I studied his ability to use his body off the dribble— the spin move off the dribble—and the best way to throw a bounce pass. I always admired Magic's cross-court bounce passes. I wondered how he was able to throw them and eventually learned. The secret was the backspin he put on the ball, which allowed him to zip the ball through the defense and have it bounce up softly into a striding teammate's hands. The other key to his passing game was anticipation. Magic would throw passes before people would even realize that they were open. He could do that because he could read defenses and see plays as they were unfolding. He left teammates in perfect positions to score—and defenses dumbfounded.

KAREEM ABDUL-JABBAR

Kareem says he remembers meeting me when I was two

He and my dad were friendly, and one time, when my dad, who was playing for the San Diego Clippers, finished a game, he passed me over to Kareem. And, for whatever reason, Kareem says he remembers holding me high up over his head and playing with me. I don't remember that, but I do remember writing a book report on him in seventh grade. In researching that paper, I learned everything about him, from his days at Power Memorial to UCLA, Milwaukee, and L.A. He had a really interesting story.

At another point in time, I watched a tape he had put out, about playing in the post, and used some of the drills that I learned from it. So when he joined our staff, I talked to him a lot about historical happenings. We talked about playing with Oscar, fighting against those Celtics teams, plays that they ran in L.A. under Pat Riley. We talked a lot.

MUHAMMAD ALI

MUHAMMAD ALI IS AN ICON.

I learned a lot from studying and watching Muhammad. One of the main takeaways was that you have to work hard in the dark to shine in the light. Meaning: It takes a lot of work to be successful, and people will celebrate that success, will celebrate that flash and hype. Behind that hype, though, is dedication, focus, and seriousness—all of which outsiders will never see. If you stop being dedicated to the craft, the commercials and contracts will all fade away.

Muhammad was also great at game planning. One of his strategies that I emulated was the rope-a-dope. A lot of people know that as a catchphrase, but I appreciate the psychology behind it, the idea that you can manipulate an opponent's strength and use it against them. That's really a brilliant concept, and one that I used often.

BILL RUSSELL

You don't win 11 rings by accident.

I knew there was a reason Bill Russell had more rings than fingers. Years ago, then, I picked up an autobiography of his and devoured it. There were a lot of valuable lessons in there. There's one anecdote Bill shared that stuck with me. He recounts how people always said he wasn't a good ball handler, just didn't know how to handle and shoot the ball. He said sure, he could do all of those things, but why would he lead the fastbreak when Bob Cousy was playing with him? Why would he shoot jumpers when Sam Jones was on his wing? The message was that if you want to win championships, you have to let people focus on what they do best while you focus on what you do best. For him, that was rebounding, running the floor, and blocking shots.

I thought that teaching was simple, yet profound. It was an insight I had never heard from anyone before. Pretty much as soon as I read that, I reached out to Bill and started a relationship and mentorship that opened up my world.

BYRON SCOTT

WE USED TO SIT NEXT TO EACH OTHER ON THE BUS.

During my rookie season, Byron and I would talk. A lot. He would share veteran stories with me, tell me about Magic, Kareem, and series they played together. He shared a lot of historical knowledge with me. He also gave me the low-down on how to cover certain shooting guards. Specifically, he worked with me on how to chase players around screens and other tactical elements of NBA defense. Outside of that, Byron schooled me on time management—how to make the most of each and every day.

When Byron came back to coach the Lakers in the last years of my career, we were like brothers. We picked up our conversations and relationship right where we had left off. Suffice to say, it was great to have him back on the same sideline.

A GOOD COACH IS OF THE UTMOST IMPORTANCE.

Coaches are teachers. Some coaches—lesser coaches—try telling you things. Good coaches, however, teach you how to think and arm you with the fundamental tools necessary to execute properly. Simply put, good coaches make sure you know how to use both hands, how to make proper reads, how to understand the game. Good coaches tell you where the fish are, great coaches teach you how to find them. That's the same at every level.

In certain situations, like in the midst of a game, good coaches relay executional information. They point out what specifically is and isn't working. Based on that and your own feel for the game, you utilize some of that information immediately and you save some of it in your back pocket for crucial moments during the game. Then, when the time is right . . . boom!

PHIL JACKSON WAS MORE THAN JUST A COACH— HE WAS A VISIONARY.

Whereas his assistant coach Tex Winter was all about the minutiae (see the following page), Phil was about the scale. He taught concepts within basketball, but more so the macro concept of basketball. He was able to teach—without lecturing—the importance of being a team and how to get from Point A to Point B to Point Championship. He was also able to get guys to understand energy, flow, and meditation.

We had a great relationship and, obviously, won a lot of games and made Purple and Gold history together. One of the reasons our relationship worked is because, in a lot of ways, we were polar opposites. Every team needs either a confrontational star player or coach. In San Antonio, Gregg Popovich was that guy and Tim Duncan was not. In Golden State, Draymond Green is the confrontational one; Steve Kerr is not. For us, Phil was not that type of person, so I provided that force. You always have to have that balance and counterbalance, and Phil and I were perfectly suited for each other in that way.

However, it took us until our second stint together to realize how we were perfectly suited for one another. During our first go together, Phil thought I was uncoachable. He thought I questioned his authority and questioned his plans. He thought I didn't listen. When he came back, he realized that was just me being me. He realized that I was just very inquisitive and unafraid to ask questions. He realized that that's how I process information and learn. Once he put his pulse on that, he was more patient with me. He was more willing to sit and answer my many questions and talk everything through.

Now, I coach my daughter's team, and we run the triangle offense. Recently, I called Phil and filled him in on what I was teaching the girls. He was surprised by how much I learned from him. More than that, he was surprised how much detail I had retained and was now passing down.

TEX WINTER WAS A BASKETBALL GENIUS.

I learned an incalculable amount from him. Tex, specifically, taught the process of the game. He taught the pure craft of it. He focused on the details, flow, and nuances of the game. He was able to bring the littlest details to life and show their ultimate importance.

He was also exceedingly patient. In our first year together in L.A., he and I would re-watch every single game together—preseason, regular season, playoffs. That's a lot of basketball. That's also detail, teaching, and patience. That's Tex. He had a great mind, and a great mind for basketball. Coaches like him are rare, and I'm blessed I got the chance to study with him.

I ALWAYS SAID LUKE WALTON WAS DESTINED TO BE A COACH.

Luke was a very smart player. He also had certain coaching traits: a bad back, like Phil used to have, and hippie lineage. I used to tell him that all the time. He didn't find it as funny as I did.

For real though, Luke had a great feel for the game. He understood how to look at it in sequences, versus looking at one play at a time, and he was able to communicate very clearly. When I looked at the amalgamation of those things, I could see he was going to be a really good coach.

T'D UP

I used to get my fair share of technical fouls. Still, I had a great relationship with the majority of referees. That's due in large part to the mutual respect we had for one another. I always made sure to talk with them, build a dialogue and rapport. That way if I talked back or pointed something out, it often held weight with them. At the least, it was better than if I only spoke to them when I was complaining.

During my last season, it was awesome going around the league and seeing each official for the last time. We would talk, laugh about old times, and share memories. I have a lot of admiration for those men and women.

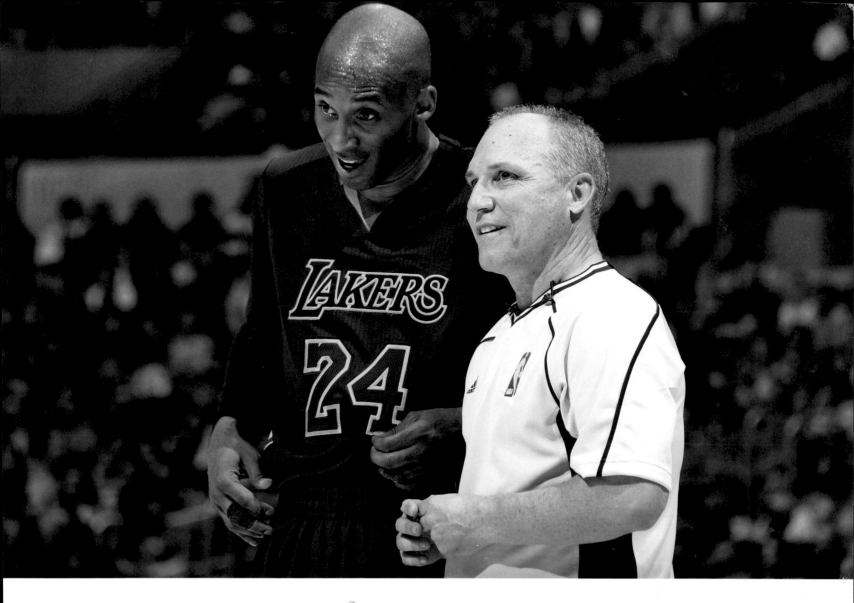

REFS HAVE A DIFFICULT JOB.

They're not just responsible for observing and moderating the action in front of them at a fast pace. They're also responsible for bearing the brunt of the emotions of a game that tend to boil over. On top of that, they're not robots, so they also have to be aware of their own emotions and try to remain objective.

It's a tough job. If refs make a mistake, they'll get lambasted. If they do a great job, no one mentions them. I always tried to keep that in mind and treat them like the real underappreciated and emotional humans that they are. I think that always worked to my benefit.

READING IS FUNDAMENTAL.

I made a point of reading the referee's handbook. One of the rules I gleaned from it was that each referee has a designated slot where he is supposed to be on the floor. If the ball, for instance, is in place W, referees X, Y, and Z each have an area on the court assigned to them.

When they do that, it creates dead zones, areas on the floor where they can't see certain things. I learned where those zones were, and I took advantage of them. I would get away with holds, travels, and all sorts of minor violations simply because I took the time to understand the officials' limitations.

PLAYING THROUGH THE PAIN

This was right after I hurt my finger on December 11, 2009. Gary was assessing, trying to gauge how bad it was. Pretty much right away, we went back into the bowels of the arena, had it X-rayed, and Gary told me it was fractured. I said, "Alright, cool, now get me back out there."

Gary looked at me like I was crazy.

I asked him, "Is it going to get better?" He said no. I said, "Exactly, there's nothing we can do about it now and it can't get worse, so tape it up and let's go."

From that point forward, we would apply a splint, which was like a hard cast at the bottom and top portion of my finger. Then we would wrap it over and over again with a spongy elastic tape. The ball would, physically, still hurt when it hit my finger. But mentally, I knew I had protection absorbing some of the pain and I could play through the rest.

We did that, literally, every time out on the court. Shoot-around, practice, game. I mean, every time out.

I HAD TO CHANGE MY SHOOTING FORM.

After I injured my right index finger in the 2009–2010 season (see previous page), I knew my usual method would no longer work. Up until then, I'd always shot off of my first two fingers. After I hurt it, I had to start focusing on using my middle finger. The middle became my point of release, and I had to sort of let my index finger drift.

Making that change took a couple of practices. Not average practices, though. Days flooded with mental and physical work. I had to mentally download the software that was the new form, and then drill it in. I definitely got my one thousand makes in on each of those days.

People ask me if the change impacted my shot, if it made me a better or worse shooter. I can't answer that. I can say that there are times when my index finger just went numb, when it had no feeling in it at all. I can also say that was still good enough to win another championship—and that's the only thing that matters.

I TORE MY ACHILLES.

This was April 12, 2013. We had just three minutes to go in a game with the Warriors. I realized right away that it was torn. First, I felt it, and then I looked down and saw it curling up the back of my leg. Still, I tried to walk on it, tried to figure out how to play around it. It became evident fast, though, that I should take the free throws and get the hell out of there.

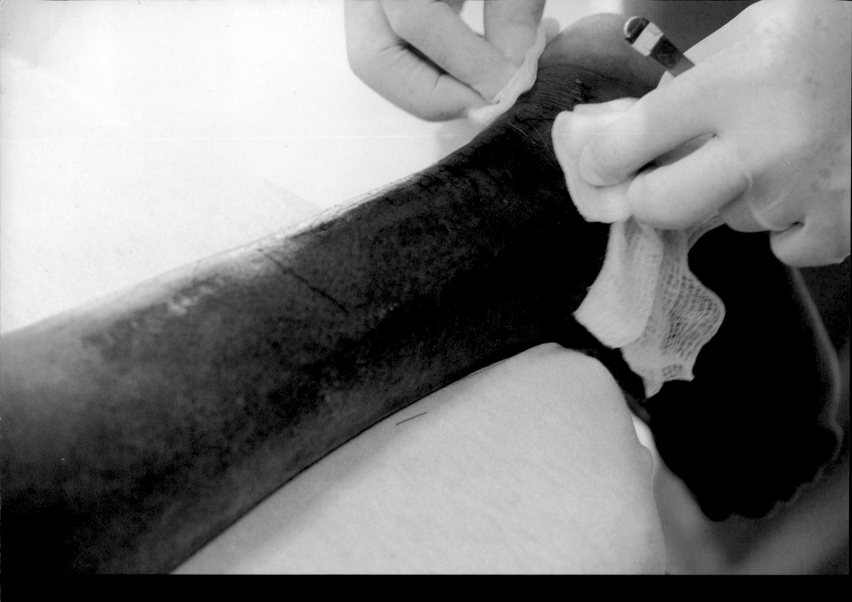

THE ACHILLES INJURY WAS MY PERSONAL MOUNT EVEREST.

Right after I sustained the injury in 2013, as I was walking off the court, I just looked at my wife and shook my head. She could immediately tell it was very serious.

I went straight to the training table in the locker room. Gary Vitti was there, so was Patrick Soon-Shiong, a surgeon and minority owner of the team (and who today owns the Los Angeles Times). We started speaking and Patrick said, "There's a new procedure and it looks very promising, but it operates on the premise that you can't

I said, "Let's do it." It was as simple as that. We started game planning for surgery the next morning right there and then. Shortly thereafter, my family came in and I talked with them. We cried about it, and I answered all my kids' questions. I assured them that Daddy was going to be fine. I remember, sometime after that, showering with crutches and being careful not to slip. I talked to the media, and I had surgery the very next day.

Before the Achilles injury, I was thinking about my career arc. I could feel my body wearing out and I knew I was on the clock. When the Achilles injury happened, I treated it as a new challenge. People were saying I might not be able to come back, but I knew I was not going to let it beat me. I was not going to let an injury dictate my retirement; I was going to dictate my retirement. That's when I decided I

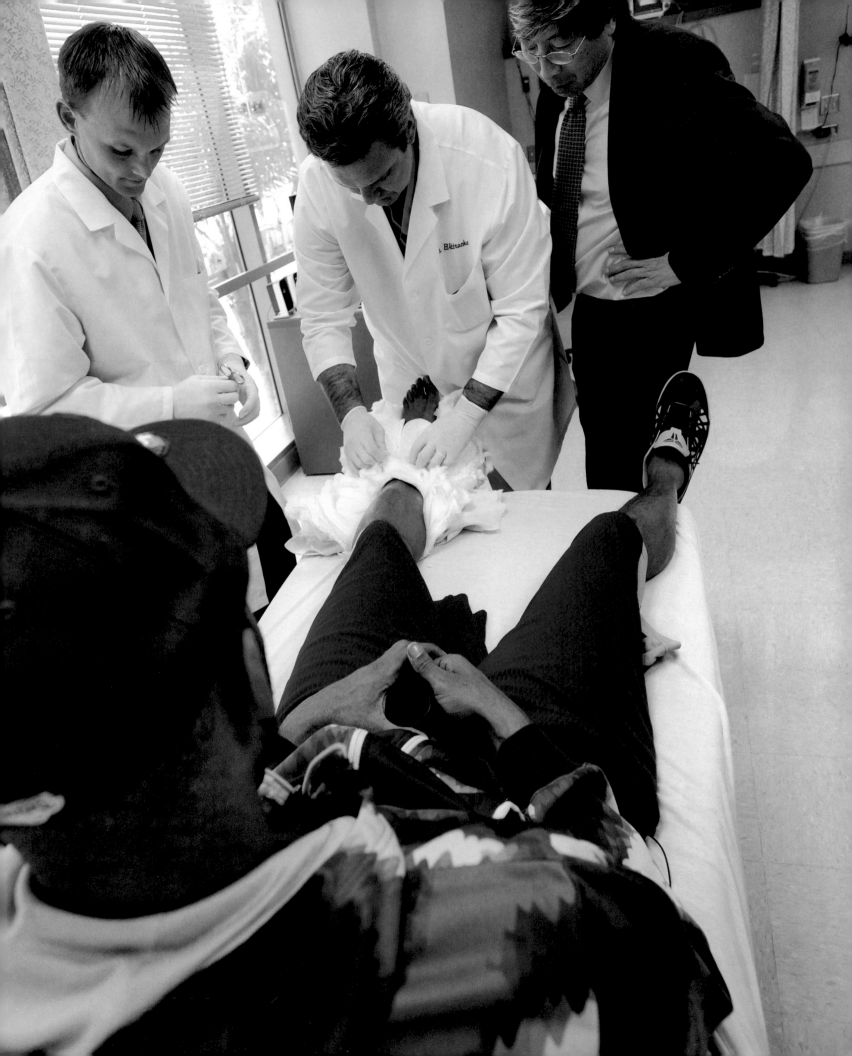

I TOOK THE DESIGN OF MY NIKES VERY SERIOUSLY.

Again, it goes back to craft and detail. For some players, sneakers were all about looks and shine. For me, it was always about peak performance. It was about the fact that I was on my feet for 48 minutes a night and relied on them to do my job.

I was an absolute perfectionist about the technology that went into my signature sneakers. I cared about every little detail. I cared about the weight, the weight distribution, the materials, the cut, the traction, the durability. I was meticulous about every curve, contour, and stitch. I didn't want any loose ends. I didn't want my foot sliding in the shoe. I didn't want anything that could take my focus, even for an instant, off the game. My sneakers didn't just have to be comfortable, they had to help me perform better.

Nike, fortunately, loved that kind of challenge. Each signature shoe improved on the one before it. We were always getting better, always striving for innovation and greatness. Always looking ahead.

AN EVOLUTIONARY REVOLUTION

In 2008, I decided I wanted my next signature sneaker to be a low top. When I told Nike that, at first they said no. I responded, "You can't say no. Phil Knight's mantra was 'Listen to the voice of the athlete.' I'm the athlete, and I want a low-cut shoe."

I got the idea from watching *futbol*. Those guys put even more torque on their ankles and lower legs than basketball players, and they were wearing boots cut even lower than our sneakers. I realized if they could do it, we for sure could. And we did.

The Kobe IV changed the game. I remember having to go in front of Foot Locker and pitch them on the Kobe IV, because they weren't sure how to sell it. It was past time for the change, though. The fallacy of a high top was that players believed it protected your ankles. In actuality, it weakens them and saps mobility.

KEEP IT REAL.

When I was young, my mindset was image, image, image.
I took that approach with the media. As I became more
experienced I realized: No matter what, people are going
to like you or not like you. So be authentic, and let them
like you or not for who you actually are. At that point,
I started keeping all of my answers blunt and straight-
forward. I would mix in some humor and sarcasm, too. I
think fans and reporters came to appreciate that, came to
appreciate the real me.

THE BIG UNKNOWNS

My routine with Team USA, compared to my NBA routine, was inconsistent. I tried to stick to my regular road workouts, but the big unknown was always the environment. During the NBA season, I knew how every city and stadium operated, which made it easier for me to visualize everything from the bus ride to the final buzzer.

When you go to China, Spain, the UK, Turkey, you don't know what the bus to the game is going to look like, you don't know what the training room is going to look like, and you don't know the layout of the arenas. Those details tend to vary, so I had to adjust accordingly.

Mentally, though, I approached national team games with the utmost intensity. I knew I was playing against guys I had never faced before, and I knew I was going to defend the other country's best player, so I locked in. I studied a lot of film and tried to figure out who my opponents were. The last thing I wanted to do was risk stepping out blindly against an unknown-but-great player. Preparation was critical.

COACH K AND I BECAME CLOSE WHEN I WAS IN HIGH SCHOOL.

I gained a lot of respect for him as he recruited me, and I would have attended Duke had I gone to college. Getting to play for him over a decade later with Team USA was fulfilling.

A few things about him stood out. For one, he was really intense, which I could appreciate. Outside of that, he really cares about and loves his players. Most of all, his competitive spirit resonated with me. He and I approach winning and losing the same way, in that winning is the goal, and losing is, well, losing isn't even on the table.

Our nation means so much to Coach Mike Krzyzewski. He really hammered home the significance of getting to represent our country. Everything he did—from having generals come to speak with us, having soldiers be a part of our preparation process, having us take tours of national monuments—was aimed at increasing our admiration and love for America. You could sense that in the way he had us playing, in the intensity we showed.

I ALWAYS AIMED TO KILL THE OPPOSITION.

The main thing LeBron and I discussed was what constitutes a killer mentality. He watched how I approached every single practice, and I constantly challenged him and the rest of the guys.

I remember there was one half when we were messing around. I came into the locker room at half-time and asked the guys—in a less PG manner—what in the hell we were doing. In the second half, LeBron responded in a big way—he came out with a truly dominant mindset. And I've seen him lead that way ever since.

WHEN I WAS ON THE NATIONAL TEAM, I COULD FOCUS ON WHAT I WANTED TO.

With the talent we had, I knew I didn't have to worry about offense. I knew I didn't have to stress over scoring. I was able to single-mindedly focus, like I'd always yearned to, on playing defense. It let me focus on putting opponents in straitjackets and erasing them from the game.

Playing with other great players, in that sense, was fun. D Wade and I would always talk about the technique of stealing the ball. He was great at reading passing lanes, and I was great at locking down on the ball, so I would force my man into the corner while D Wade would look to pick off the pass.

I had never played with a player like that before. I played with a lot of length and guys who suited my game, but I never played with a guard that explosive. Man, it was fun to hunt with D Wade.

I WAS ONE OF THE ELDER STATESMEN ON OUR NATIONAL TEAMS.

I already had three rings, had just gotten to the Finals, and was poised to go back again. From that perspective, I was the alpha in the locker room. I didn't really pick anyone else's brain. If anything, because I was so much more experienced, other guys would approach me about incorporating aspects of my game into theirs.

For the most part, we discussed executional elements of basketball, because the international game is played differently. I had an edge because I grew up playing in Italy, so I would help guys adjust how they were processing the action and our schemes.

MY PROCESS WITH TEAM USA WAS DIFFERENT FROM MOST OF THE OTHER GUYS'.

Most players listen to music every game. They have their headphones on religiously and use music to get them in the right state of mind. They'd even sing and dance. I rarely ever did that. Sometimes, even when I had headphones on, there wasn't any music playing. It was a feint to keep people away, and to get in my zone. For the most part, before games I just liked being there, hearing the sounds of the environment and observing everything.

I'm trying to feel the energy of the environment.

I made every second of the national anthem count. During those precious moments, I'm hearing all the little sounds and imbibing the energy of the arena. I'm taking the opportunity to be aware of what's going on, to be aware of the teammates around me, the basket in front of me, the basket behind me, all the other sounds and objects. It's a full concentration and understanding of the arena.

In essence, I'm trying to feel the energy of the environment and allow it to move through me. That then propels me and fuels me to have a great performance.

I've done that since I was a kid sort of naturally. I never put too much thought into it. When Phil Jackson came, though, I started to understand the importance of my personalized meditative process. From then on, I placed an increased emphasis on it.

I WOULDN'T SAY MY LEADERSHIP STYLE CHANGED OVER THE YEARS.

I liked challenging people and making them uncomfortable. That's what leads to introspection and that's what leads to improvement. You could say I dared people to be their best selves.

That approach never wavered. What I did adjust, though, was how I varied my approach from player to player. I still challenged everyone and made them uncomfortable, I just did it in a way that was tailored to them. To learn what would work and for who, I started doing homework and watched how they behaved. I learned their histories and listened to what their goals were. I learned what made them feel secure and where their greatest doubts lay. Once I understood them, I could help bring the best out of them by touching the right nerve at the right time.

At the beginning of our first championship run, Tex Winter put me in charge of the triangle offense.

He made me—young me—the de facto leader on the court. Some guys chafed when they heard me calling the shots, and I couldn't have cared less. My philosophy was, Tex Winter—*the* Tex Winter—put me in control, and if you don't like it, if you don't like me calling you out for not being in the correct spot, tough.

Once guys understood my motivation, they started to fall in line. As I got older, they didn't even need to understand why—they instinctively followed. They knew what my goals for the team were, and they knew what I was trying to do.

In my final years, I was really hard on D'Angelo Russell, Jordan Clarkson, Larry Nance, Jr., my younger teammates. I was trying to use my 20 years of experience to expedite their growth. Now, a few years later, it's gratifying to see that Jordan is wearing my number in Cleveland. That shows me they really internalized and understood my motivations and hopes for them.

THE LAKERS ARE A FAMILY.

I looked up to a lot of Laker greats, a lot of the players who came before me and created the franchise's mystique and lore. James Worthy, Byron Scott, Elgin Baylor, to name a few. It's like an exclusive fraternity. There are a lot of historical jewels in the family, and those jewels get passed down from generation to generation.

The OG greats, though, won't hang around you if you don't display the same passion as they do. They won't share their time and memories with you if you don't display the same effort and drive for excellence that they did.

Even though I was only 17 when I became a Laker, I felt like a member of the family from day one. I think I was accepted so quickly because everyone saw how hard I worked, saw how badly I wanted to fulfill my destiny and return L.A. to its championship ways.

THE MAMBA
MENTALITY

Initially, I thought the phrase "Mamba Mentality" was just a catchy hashtag that I'd start on Twitter. Something witty and memorable. But it took off from there and came to symbolize much more.

The mindset isn't about seeking a result—it's more about the process of getting to that result. It's about the journey and the approach. It's a way of life. I do think that it's important, in all endeavors, to have that mentality.

Whether I hear an elite college or NBA player or a Fortune 500 CEO reference the #MambaMentality, I find it very meaningful. When I see people talk about finding inspiration in it, it makes all of my hard work, all of the sweat, all of the 3 AM wakeups feel worth it. That's why I put together this book. All these pages incorporate lessons—not just lessons on basketball, but also on the Mamba Mentality.

DRAFT

A TEACHING MOMENT

My balance, as a young player, is off.

Just look at the dichotomy between us, starting with posture. Michael is standing straight from the waist up. He's not leaning in either direction, and because of that he is balanced and centered. He is in control of his body, and the play.

Compare all that to my defense. Now, I'm using my forearm to thrust weight into his back, just like they teach it. Unfortunately, that's about all I'm doing right. I'm leaning forward, which is a major no-no, and putting too much pressure on him. That alone, by dint of gravity, causes me to be off-balance. As a result, one move by Michael, one decisive spin right or feint left, would throw me off and give him room to either shoot or spin off of me. This defense is definitely *no bueno*.

Thankfully, I actually saw this photo back in 1998. After studying it, I corrected my posture and balance. After that, it was a lot harder to operate against me in the post.

PRESSURE

I never felt outside pressure. I knew what I wanted to accomplish, and I knew how much work it took to achieve those goals. I then put in the work and trusted in it. Besides, the expectations I placed on myself were higher than what anyone expected from me.

SOMETIMES YOU HAVE TO PUT THE TEAM ON YOUR BACK.

Shaq was out, and we were going through a rough patch. We had lost two games in a row going into this one, so we had to get out of that funk. For us to do that, I knew I'd have to carry the load from both a scoring and emotional perspective.

This dunk, which happened in the third quarter, was a statement. Each of my 52 points was important—the game went into double overtime—but this is the bucket that set the tone. It was me throwing down the gauntlet and telling my teammates we were going to win, we were going to right the ship. And we won. In fact, we won nine of the next 10 games.

That's not to say it was easy. This was my sixth straight night of scoring 40 points, and my body was feeling it. After this game, my knee swelled up to the size of a melon. I was having a lot of trouble moving, and we had a game in Utah the next night. Still, I suited up, put on a brace, and played 40 minutes on it. I scored 40, and more important, we won. You have to give everything to the game, to your team. That's what it takes to win. That's what it takes to be great.

A BIG SHOT IS JUST ANOTHER SHOT.

People make a huge deal out of clutch shots. Thing is, it's just one shot. If you make a thousand shots a day, it's just one of a thousand. Once you're hitting that many, what's one more? That was my mentality from day one.

This particular shot was a game-tying three in the NBA Finals. I was going to get the ball on this play, no matter what. The defense could've tried to deny me, but it would not have mattered. I was going to do whatever I had to, in this moment, to come get it.

Once you have the rock, you always have to know who is guarding you. You have to not just know, but *know*—and I knew Rip Hamilton's defensive strategy. Rip was very fundamentally sound and played you straight up. He didn't do much out of the ordinary, which can be fine. Fundamentally sound, though, was not going to stop me.

So, I sized him up, kept all that information in mind, and made him do what I wanted him to do. I dragged the ball over to the wing, rocked him back, and rose up, knowing that he would only raise his arms to contest. At that point, it's just about whether I make the shot or not.

As a team, our spacing was really good. Even if they wanted to help Rip, they would not have been able to. We would spread the floor and make sure any help defenders were a long way away. By the time they'd get over, my shot, which came off of a quick rocking motion, would've already been in the air.

The last thing you notice in the photo is the lift that I'm getting. That didn't just happen overnight. It was late in the game, and it was the Finals, but I was able to get up because I was in shape. It's a small thing, but it makes a big difference.

tHOUGH MY EYES AND HEAD
ARE POINTED
STRAIGHT AHEAD —

MY FEET ARE
STARTING TO
VEER LEFT.

FOOTWORK IS ABOUT EFFICIENCY.

I needed to be able to get to my attack spots in one or two dribbles. I also needed to be able to shoot from range. In doing so, I limited the amount of time I gave the defense to react, conserved my energy, and forced them to pick me up a great distance from the basket. The key was knowing how to move the defense with just my feet and my eyes and the positioning of my body, by knowing how to manipulate them left or right without having to put the ball on the floor.

During my early years in the NBA, I was surprised to learn that I took a different, more fundamental and serious, approach to footwork than a lot of players. A lot of players solely focused on improving off the dribble, but I also always placed added emphasis on playing off the catch. I learned that approach when I was young, in Europe. There, our practices included scrimmages where we weren't allowed to dribble. So later, when I moved to the States, I had all of the footwork down from those

days. Only after mastering pivots—reverse pivots, inside reverse pivots, outside reverse pivots—did I work on the sexier between-the-legs, behind-the-backs, and crossovers.

Later in my career, players asked me to share the how-tos of some of my footwork with them. LeBron, Durant, Westbrook—they really wanted to know the intricacies of it. The timing of their enthusiasm was perfect for me: I was on the last stretch of my career, and we weren't competing for championships, so I was happy to share what I knew.

GOD GAVE US TWO HANDS.

As a kid, I'm talking six years old, it bothered me when something felt like a weakness. So I worked really hard on my left hand at that age. Specifically, I would brush my teeth with my left hand; I would write my name with my left hand. I hated the feeling of being uncomfortable.

That's how I looked at it on the court, too. That's why I felt it was so important to be able to use both of them equally. Whether dribbling or shooting, pivoting or spinning, it was important to me that I felt comfortable with either hand.

NEW YORK KNICKS, December 9, 2003

I NEVER SHIED AWAY FROM CONTACT.

I definitely knew I was stronger than Reggie Miller. I don't know if it was a mental thing, but I was more of a bully than him.

I would get to the basket, and try to attack it as much as I could. When you go to the basket like that, you're not using your arms as much as you are your body. You use that to create separation. A lot of times, with a lot of guys, the defensive player becomes the attacker and the offensive player capitulates to that. I never approached it that way. When I went to the basket, I was attacking and I wasn't the one at risk of getting hurt: they were. Whether you're Reggie or Shaq, I'm going to the basket hard and making you think twice about whether you want to contest it.

THIS WAS FUN.

Look at Dennis. He's holding the crap out of me, but he knew how to get away with that. He had all sorts of little tricks that you couldn't decipher on TV. You couldn't see how he was holding or pushing or grabbing. Even if you could see it, TV didn't do it justice. He's one of the smartest basketball players I've ever played against or with. He was, truly, a master of the game within the game.

Michael used to do the same thing. He would shove me into screens and hold my jersey. I learned from those guys, from those Bulls, what it takes to win a championship.

Understanding the importance of contact and physicality is only half the battle. You have to love it, and I did. You had to love having your jersey held and holding their jersey back. You had to love getting hit once so you could hit them back twice. You had to love every last push, shove, and elbow. Understand and embrace that mentality. Once you do, you are ready to win.

In a situation like this, you also have to understand that the screener is always the threat. When preparing for a team that runs a lot of screens or pick-and-rolls, you don't study the ball handler or the player who runs off of the pick. You have to study the person setting the screens. That person, the screener, is the real threat.

The easiest way to understand what to expect is by watching film and learning how individual players like to set screens, because everyone does it differently. Once you know that—where on the court they like to set it, the timing, the angle—you can start plotting an offensive defense to get around them and negate their screen.

So, what would I do differently than in this photo? I would not lay on the screen. I would not try pushing off of Dennis. By doing that, I gave him access to my arms, which allowed him to tie my arms up and hold me. Instead of laying on the screen, I'd keep my distance from Dennis, and deal with Michael before he got there.

PUSH F INTO DENNIS
ONLY GAVE HIM ACCESS
TO TIE UP MY ARMS—

HE WOULD GRAB IN WAYS
NO ONE COULD SEE.

SHAQ WAS DOMINANT.
THERE'S NO QUESTION ABOUT THAT.

Even when you're playing with a dominant center, the best way to get them rolling is by creating easy opportunities for them. I did that by selling the idea that I was going to shoot the ball. That would draw defenders' attention to me and away from Shaq. His finish would then be simple.

So how did I go about that?

I would attack. I would penetrate. I would get all the way to the rim. I would even leave my feet—which is fundamentally unsound—to make the defender believe I was going to try to finish. Once they bought in, I would scoop the ball off to Shaq.

All of this is fairly obvious, but the subtle secret to success is to get defenders to put their hands in the air in an attempt to block your shot. If you do that, if you really fool them into thinking they need to contest, there's always a nice open pocket to shovel a pass through.

Let's talk about the pass, too. If you're going to go through all of that effort to set the play up, if you're going to get hacked and pounded on your way to the hoop, you better make sure you don't mess up the last step. You have to know your big man's preferences. You have to know where they like to sit in the lane, how they like to catch the ball, which hand they like to finish with.

On this play, I just had to make sure to put the pass on Shaq's left hand. Then he could use his body as a shield against the trailing defender and complete the play without worrying about getting fouled.

SEATTLE SUPERSONICS, April 15, 2002

SETTING A TIGHTROPE

No matter what was going on between us, everyone on our team knew that Shaq and I were good for 30-plus points and 10-plus rebounds/assists every night. That knowledge provided them with a sense of security, but it could also lull them into complacency.

In an effort to stave that off, Shaq and I would, conscious of the intermittent tension around us, ratchet that up. By doing so, our teammates would lock in and raise their own level of competitiveness.

It's worth understanding, though, that it was never about us. It was never about Shaq and Kobe. It was about making sure our teammates were fully invested and understood the seriousness of what we were trying to do. It was about making sure they understood they were walking a tightrope, and Shaq and I were not always going to be their safety nets.

Shaq was a special player. He understood both how to use his body and mind. He understood both angles and human nature. He understood intimidation and domination.

The one thing I specifically picked up from Shaq was his physicality, his brute force. Despite being a guard, I wanted players to be sore, to be beat up, after guarding me for 48 minutes. That would give me the mental advantage the next time we matched up. After Shaq left, in the spirit of that, I played more in the post and dealt out some serious punishment to guards around the league.

YOU HAD TO MOVE HIM.

When we went up against Shaq-led teams, the plan of attack was always to move him around. We wanted to put him in screen-and-roll actions, and, more important, put him off of the ball and make him become the guy who needs to make full defensive rotations. We felt like that would exploit some of his weaknesses.

When it came time to attack Shaq at the rim one-on-one, I would just build up a head of steam and go right at him. He would see that coming and foul me every time instead of risk getting dunked on. So I knew I would shoot two free throws every time I went at him.

L: SAN ANTONIO SPURS, February 3, 2005. R: HOUSTON ROCKETS, January 7, 2005

WHEN FUNDAMENTALS ARE NO LONGER FUNDAMENTAL

When Caron Butler and I were on the Lakers together, we clicked immediately. He would come to my house all the time; he would work out with me all the time. We would play one-on-one before and after practice. We would really push each other. In time, he adopted a lot of my footwork. You could see it, once he was traded, in his pull-up jumpers and turnarounds in the post.

It was really hard for me when he got traded. I had invested a lot of time in him that summer, and we worked together constantly. I thought he was poised to have a breakout year for us.

I thought that because Caron was a great student of the game, and someone who, dating back to college, always excelled at the fundamentals. It's weird, actually—fundamentals aren't really fundamental anymore. A lot of players don't understand the game or the importance of footwork, spacing. It's to the point where if you know the basics, you have an advantage on the majority of players.

MOVE YOUR PUPPIES.

It was 2000, and I was having problems getting over screens when guarding the ball. When the All-Star Game came around, and Gary Payton and I were warming up together, I pulled him aside.

"Gary," I said, "I'm having trouble getting through screens. What do I do?"

He was a great competitor, but he took the time to walk me through his approach. He told me I had to make myself thin and, I'll never forget this, move my puppies. He explained I had to slide, not run, through the screen and to do so I had to make myself as small as I could and move my feet as quickly as possible. Almost, he explained, like a sheet of paper going through a door.

After the All-Star break, I worked on it constantly in practice. I just kept plugging away. Not coincidentally, that was the first year I made First Team All-Defensive.

KG WAS A WIZARD ON DEFENSE.

I don't think people give Kevin Garnett enough credit for that. He captained every defense he was ever part of, and had a really big voice. He also had long arms and athleticism, so he was able to command large swatches of the court as a communicator and shot-blocker.

His versatility at such a size was also startling, and, ultimately, game-changing. He could dribble, pass, and shoot. I think, honestly, we're all fortunate that Minnesota didn't surround him with an abundance of talent during his prime. If they did, it would have been a real challenge for us and San Antonio to get past them.

I WOULD TRY TO DRIVE THROUGH HIM.

KG was the leader of his team and I was the leader of mine, so I made sure to send a message to everyone in the game: I see your top dog and I am not going to back down. There were some times that I got the best of him, and there were times when he came out on top. Whatever the case may be, he and I both never backed down from a challenge, and that goes back to high school.

When it came to blocking my shots, KG would try to use his arms and length. He was aware that he didn't have a strong frame, so he wouldn't use his body, but he would definitely use his length and cover the rim and shield the rim. He would move away from me, to protect his body from contact, and to block the best angles. A lot like Bill Russell used to.

L and R: MINNESOTA TIMBERWOLVES, May 1, 2003

KG NEVER JAWED WITH ME.

More than anything, Kevin was a competitor and wanted to win. He knew that when he talked crap to some guys, it would faze them out of their game. And he knew that when he talked smack to others, they would level up. I fit in the latter category, and he knew that, so he never directed one word of trash talk to me.

In the 2008 Finals, KG and Kendrick Perkins had some success talking a bunch of trash to Pau. They tried it again in 2010, but I wasn't having it. I challenged them back, and Pau, to his credit, did the same thing. Metta World Peace also took a stand. That was a game-changer for us.

LAMAR ODOM WAS OUR GLUE.

It's easy to understate LO's role, but it's important not to. He was the ultimate teammate. He was charismatic, unselfish, and had a great sense of community. LO was the one who brought the team together, whether that was encouraging group outings, having one-on-one dinners with certain guys, or just being available to hang with.

The only thing as big as his heart was his talent. He was a superb passer, he could handle the ball, and he developed a steady jumper. I always knew I could count on him on the court. Whenever I got double-teamed, my initial instinct was always to find him and let him make the right play.

During our title runs in 2009 and 2010, every player on the team had a role. Pau, for example, was the intellectual; Derek was the big brother. Lamar Odom, then, was the cool-ass uncle who took care of everybody and always came through in the clutch.

UTAH JAZZ, April 2, 2010

A CRITICAL PERIOD FOR MY DEVELOPMENT

At the end of my first season in the NBA, we had made it to the Semifinals, up against Utah. But in the deciding fifth game, I let fly four airballs, and we lost our chance at the title. Those shots let me know what I needed to work on the most: my strength. That's all the airballs did for me.

In that game, nerves weren't the problem. I just wasn't strong enough to get the ball there. My legs were spaghetti; they couldn't handle that long of a season. How did I respond to that? By getting on an intense weight-training program. By the start of the next season, my legs and arms were stronger and I was ready to get it on.

In the immediate aftermath, I was never concerned by how the franchise or fans would react. I knew I would put in the work, which is what I did. In fact, as soon as we landed I went to the Pacific Palisades high school gym and shot all night long. I went back the next day and worked. And I worked and worked and worked. In my mind, it was never a matter of, "Oh, no, I'll never get another shot at this." I felt that my destiny was already written. I felt—I knew—that my future was undeniable and no one, not a person or a play, could derail it.

IN 2003 IT WAS A WRAP FOR EVERYBODY.

There was nothing—emotionally, mentally, physically, strategically—anyone could do that season to stop me.

Once I reached that level, health aside, there was nothing anyone could do during the ensuing years to slow me down. At that point, it was about the Lakers surrounding me with enough talent that we could be in contention and challenge for the championship.

For some people, I guess, it might be hard to stay sharp once you've reached the pinnacle. Not for me, though. It was never enough. I always wanted to be better, wanted more. I can't really explain it, other than that I loved the game but had a very short memory. That fueled me until the day I hung up my sneakers.

L: SACRAMENTO KINGS, April 10, 2003. R: L.A. CLIPPERS, October 23, 2003, Away

ALLEN IVERSON WAS SMALL, BUT HE WAS ALSO INCREDIBLE.

My philosophy was to use my height advantage and shoot over the top of him. I don't need to try anything, I don't need to go anywhere, I don't need to try to back him down. I'll just shoot over him, because I can get a clean look.

What I'm talking about is not the same as settling for a jumper. When Allen was covering me, I'd receive the ball in favorable locations, in attacking positions like the mid-post, because he couldn't stop me from catching a pass.

But couldn't I have caught it even closer, maybe in the post? Couldn't I have taken him off the dribble from 25 feet out? Maybe, but that wouldn't have been smart.

I chose not to catch the ball in the post, because the Sixers would have just fronted and trapped me. I could have squared up and dribbled, but they would have helped and trapped in that situation, too. By catching it on the elbow or mid-wing, I mitigate all of these schemes, because they couldn't front me on the pass and I didn't need to dribble to get an open look over the top of him.

COVERING ALLEN WAS ALL ABOUT TIMING.

When I went head-to-head with Allen, I always tried to figure out when he was going to be aggressive.

Let me backtrack for a second. Within Larry Brown's system, there was an ebb and flow to Allen's attack. The first couple of minutes, the team would get loose, move the ball, try to spread touches. Then, from around the 10-minute mark until the eight-minute mark, Allen would attack. I worked hard to decipher those patterns of attack.

Once I figured that out, I would do everything in my power to throw Allen off during those stretches. I would bump him and get physical. I would deny him the ball. I would make him catch it 30 feet from the basket. If I could do that—if I could frustrate him—it would throw off his rhythm.

Then, during stretches when Allen would otherwise be passive, I allowed him to catch the ball. After not scoring or getting anything easy during the previous few minutes, he would then be uber-assertive, and thus more susceptible to falling into traps created by our team defense. It would frustrate him even more.

The other mechanism I used to cover Allen also involved timing. In essence, I would pay attention to the amount of time it took him to go from getting the ball to attacking. If he was catching the ball and his rate was: read the defense, one-one-thousand, two-one-thousand, go—then I'd know what his clock was. The next time he'd get the ball, when I knew he was at two-one-thousand I would preemptively back up and take away his attack.

When I covered great players, they often tried covering me. That meant, when we had the ball, I would look for offensive rebounds. But with Allen, as soon as we put a shot up I would look for him, like, "Where is he?! Where is he?!" because he never matched up with me due to my size advantage. I was running over to him, jamming him up, and impeding him from getting out in transition. If you could stop Allen from gaining momentum, stop him from getting easy buckets, covering him became a much more reasonable task.

KOBE STOPPER?

Ruben Patterson and I played together for a bit, so I got to know what he could and couldn't do, and he could play defense. But I have to laugh at the whole Kobe Stopper thing he started.

I actually think he tried using it as a ploy to get a bigger contract in free agency. The idea was solid, the execution was flawed, though.

Not too long ago I told him, "You should have called me before you went ahead and said it. You should have said, 'Kob, I need a favor. I need you to say I'm the best defender you ever faced. I need you to help me get this money.'"

I would have done that for Ruben. I would have been happy to help him. After he went ahead and did it on his own, though, I had no choice but to light him up every time I saw him. No choice.

I prided myself on playing any so-called Kobe Stopper, any specialist brought in by a team to try to slow me down. When we were a championship-caliber team, other GMs were constructing their rosters to dethrone us. One of the methods they attempted was employing a Kobe Stopper, someone paid strictly to stop me. When teams did that, it was my job to make them question their ability to spot talent in the first place.

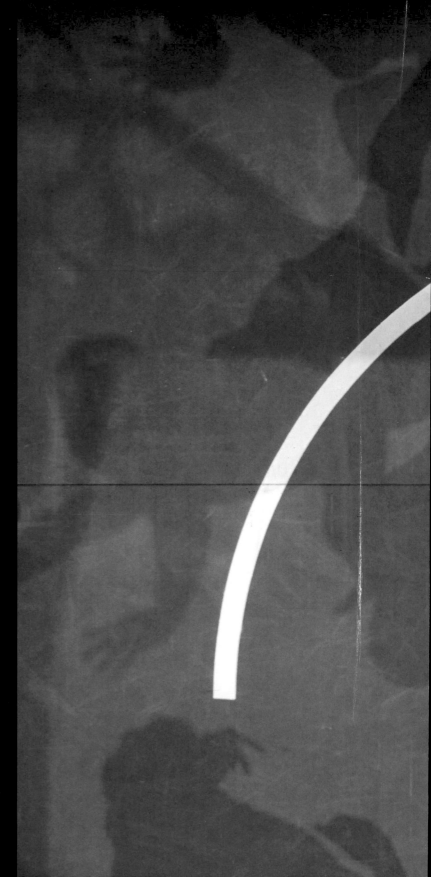

MY LEFT ARM REMINDS DIKEMBE
I AM THE THREAT

WHILE HE USES HIS
LEFT ARM TO SUBTLY
PULL ME DOWN.

DUNKING IS ABOUT DOMINATION.

When you dunk the ball, it lets the opposition know your mentality. It lets them know you're there to humiliate them. It also sets an emotional tone with your teammates. It lets them know you're going to climb mountains this game and inspires them to want to climb with you.

Now, you can't just attack the cup and hope to dunk. You have to know your own limitations. More than that, you have to know the defense. To do that, you have to study film and watch how opponents like to block shots. If you're prepared with that info—with the hand they prefer to rise up with, the situations they'll back down in—you'll know how to attack and confront them.

Dikembe Mutombo was, obviously, one of the greatest defensive players of all time. He was long and lean, and he knew what he could get away with. One of the things he was great at was using his left hand to subtly try to pull you down or at least knock you off balance in the air. That, in particular, was so crafty because it appeared fundamentally sound, but in reality he was using that hand as a weapon.

My response in that situation was simple: I had to let Dikembe know that I was the real threat and not him. So, like him, I'd use my left arm and elbow. They would create space, but more important, they'd send a message: if you come any higher, you're going to run into my arm and it won't be fun for you.

Like always, you want to be the one dishing out the punishment. And the dunks.

PHILADELPHIA 76ERS, June 10, 2001, Away

LOOK AT HAKEEM'S LEFT HAND.

He was pulling me down, just like Dikembe, with that hand. It gave him the ability to get to the ball. Pulling and shoving—that's how he blocked shots.

At the time I was thinking: I'm going up against Hakeem, this is pretty cool . . . but I'm not going to let it impact me. I also wanted to send him a message that I'm not your typical young guard who is going to complain to the refs or capitulate. I'm going to go right through your arm, your body, whatever you throw my way, because I'm a freight train.

In general, Hakeem Olajuwon was an extremely intelligent defender. He knew where guys liked to attack from, how they positioned the ball, what their patterns were. Due to that intelligence and scouting, Hakeem knew where you were going to go and how you were going to try to finish. That allowed him to pile up steals and blocks.

As an offensive player, you combat that type of mental edge by negating it. You have to know him as well or even better than he knows you. You have to know where he likes to come from, how he likes to block shots, how quickly he can recover. With that knowledge, you can be mindful of how and where to attack from.

VINCE CARTER BROUGHT OUT THE BEST IN ME.

He came into the league a few years after me and set the world on fire. That sparked the conversation of who was better: Vince or AI. I played with Shaq, so at that point I wasn't even in the conversation. I was an afterthought. Due to those loud whispers, I always had extra oomph when I played against him.

My mentality was that I was going to play him on both ends of the floor, and he was going to have help guarding me. By being able to score on offense and personally shut him down on defense, I wanted to let people know my place in that conversation wasn't even up for debate.

TORONTO RAPTORS, c. 2001

A PROBLEM YOU'RE GOING TO HAVE TO DEAL WITH

We were about to move on from the first round of the 1999 playoffs.

I remember asking Shaq if he was ready. "For what?" he questioned.

"This boy we're seeing in the next round," I replied.

"Robinson?"

"Nah, the other one."

"He's soft," said Shaq.

"I've been watching him all year," I responded, "and he's a problem that you're going to have to deal with."

Shaq sort of waved it off. By the time the Spurs were finished sweeping us, Tim Duncan had averaged something like 30 points. He was already on my radar, but after that series? Wow. I realized San Antonio would be a threat we'd have to deal with for all of eternity.

L: SAN ANTONIO SPURS, March 30, 2006. R: SAN ANTONIO SPURS, January 25, 2009

TIM DUNCAN WAS A SMART DEFENDER.

He was angular, and used it to his advantage. He also embodied the way San Antonio played defense. The Spurs fool you into believing that there is going to be contact when you drive to the basket, then—poof—there isn't. They contest shots by jumping straight up, all the time. They move away from contact, because they know that in-air contact gives the offensive player balance, but when you move away, the offender ends up off-balance. They did that as much as possible.

I realized that around 2001. They would jump with high hands, and that was now just a runway for me. I was just going to go over or through them, forget trying to draw a foul, and dunk in their faces.

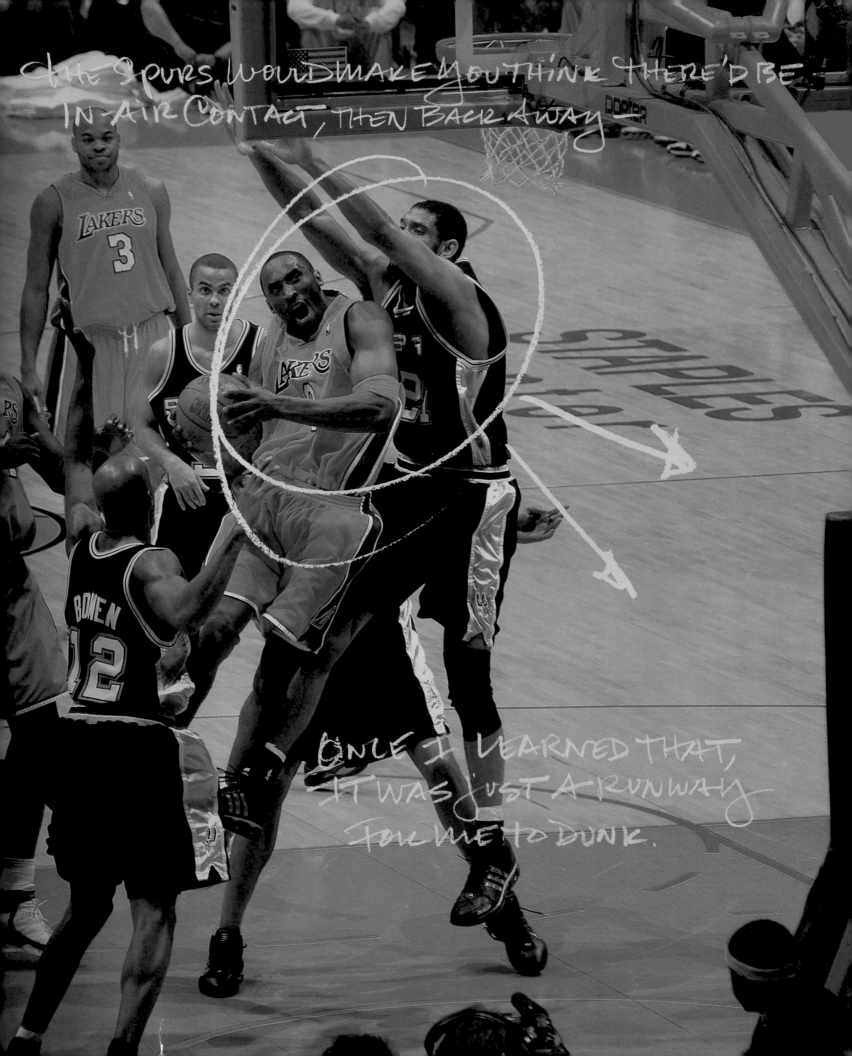

THE SPURS WOULD MAKE YOU THINK THERE'D BE
IN-AIR CONTACT, THEN BACK AWAY

ONCE I LEARNED THAT,
IT WAS JUST A RUNWAY
FOR ME TO DUNK.

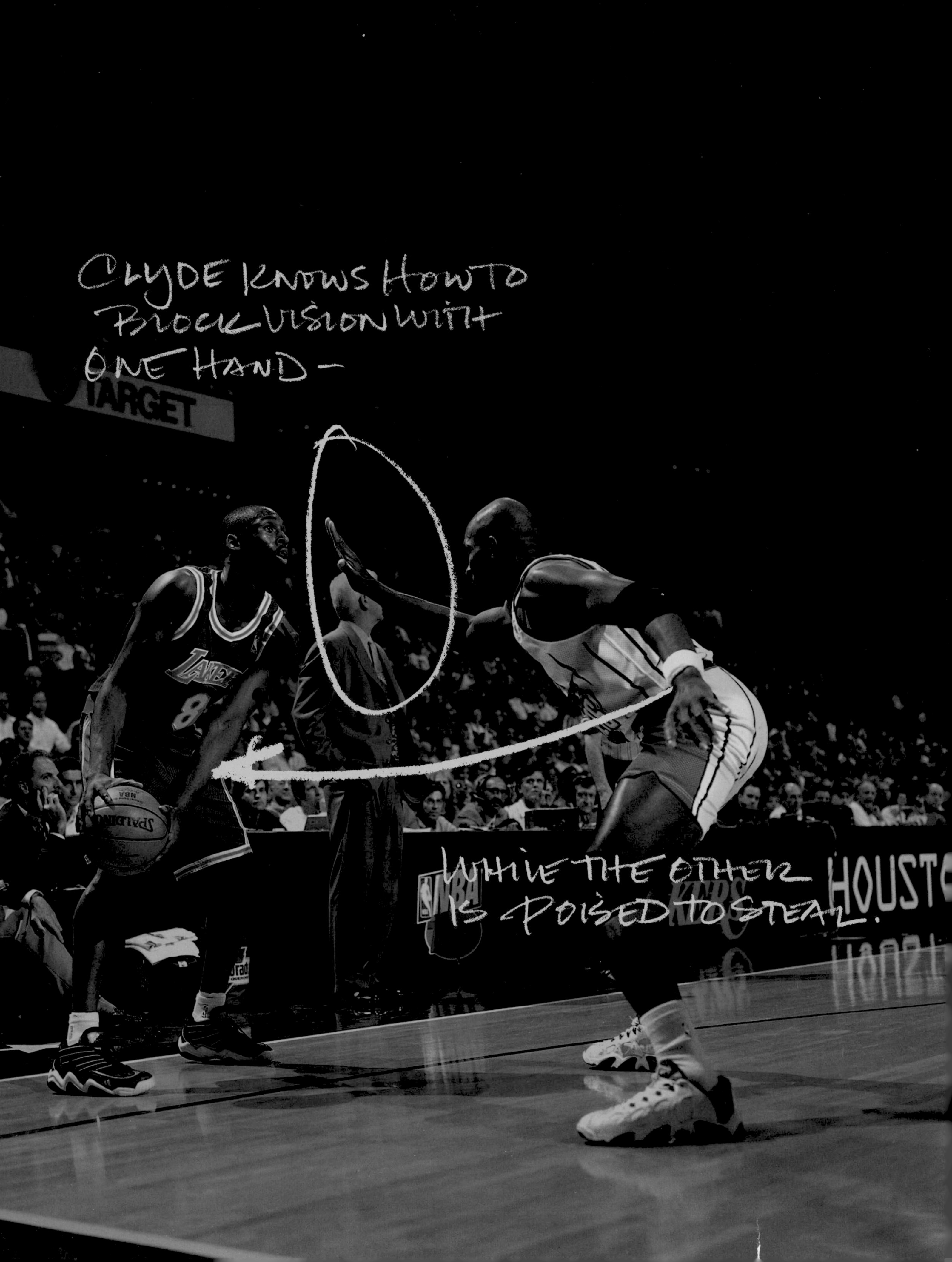

CLYDE KNOWS HOW TO
BLOCK VISION WITH
ONE HAND—

WHILE THE OTHER
IS POISED TO STEAL.

L: HOUSTON ROCKETS. 1997, Away. R: HOUSTON ROCKETS. April 1, 2004

ONE OF MY SEMINAL NBA MOMENTS

It was 1997, and we were up against the Rockets. I remember I'd had a really tough first half. I was matched up with Clyde Drexler, and I don't think I made a single shot. I came out in the second half, kicked it into high gear, and scored 27 points off the bench. That was a big moment for me.

I always admired Clyde. I always looked at how he defended. He understood how to use his hands and block the vision of the player with one hand while using the other as a threat to steal the ball, or shield it. He also had great balance and used that to his advantage. The way I defend, in fact, can be attributed to Clyde. (And MJ, of course.)

I WAS GOING TO DOMINATE.

It didn't matter who I was up against. That was my mentality going into every game. The only difference, based on who I was up against, was how would I do it.

Take Cuttino "Cat" Mobley, for example. Cat liked to use his quickness and hands a lot. At the same time, he hated when I put my body on him. That was the back-and-forth every time that we'd play. He would swipe at the ball and try to get it when it was down low, and I would use my physicality on him. I would put my weight on him, hit him with elbows, just beat him up and gain the advantage.

L and R: HOUSTON ROCKETS, October 30, 2007

TRACY MCGRADY HAD SOME MAGIC TO HIS GAME.

Tracy might have, in effect, been the hardest matchup. He could do just about everything on offense. He could go either direction and shoot or drive, he could post up and shoot over his left and right shoulders, and he was long and tall. From that standpoint, I would try to disrupt his flow by pinpointing his aggressive moments and taking those away from him.

On nights I had to cover Tracy, I tried to figure out what would make him uncomfortable, which was getting underneath him and being physical with his legs. I'd get deep into his legs, his back—which I knew he had particular insecurities about—his hips, and make him uneasy. The goal was to suffocate him and take away any daylight he might have to score.

TRACY LIKES TO CROUCH LOW AND WIDE —

MAINTAINING HIS BALANCE SO EACH HAND HAS EQUAL OPPORTUNITY TO GRAB.

TRACY ALWAYS HAD QUICK HANDS.

He was especially good at using them to swipe at the ball and knock it away. My goal, then, was to neutralize his hands as threats by keeping the ball away from him. As long as I did that, I knew I could get to the spots I wanted and dictate what kind of night I was going to have.

WE WERE ON A
COLLISION COURSE.

When Boston acquired multiple All-Stars in 2008, we knew it was going to come down to the two of us. That happened in 2008, and it happened again in 2010.

In retrospect, it was awesome to be a part of that historic rivalry. I knew the history. I knew what Jerry West went through, knew what the Showtime Lakers went through. That definitely added to the meaning of it all. At the time, though, my mindset was: They're in the way and I have to win; I have to win this title. It didn't matter that they had three future Hall-of-Famers and Rasheed Wallace and Rajon Rondo and others. It didn't matter because the history books wouldn't reflect that. The only thing that gets recorded is titles, and we had to fight our way through those guys and win one.

My LEFT FOREARM
PUTS PRESSURE INTO
PAUL'S BACK—

WHILE MY LEFT LEG
KEEPS HIM FROM
SPINNING OFF ME.

PAUL PIERCE WAS ONE OF THE TOUGHEST PLAYERS I EVER HAD TO GUARD.

He really understood how to use his body. He would use his heft to shield you, and he would use his size to shoot over you.

What I tried to do here was turn the tables and gain the positional advantage. I used my left forearm to put pressure into his back. I put my left leg behind him to further negate any opportunity he had to spin off of me. Simultaneously, I used my right leg to cut off his angle to drive directly. Then, if he made any mistake with the ball, my right hand was there to flick it away and capitalize on the error.

The best result of this play would have been to take the ball from him or block his shot. Another good result would have been to make him uncomfortable enough where he wouldn't shoot at all. It would have been OK also if he shot the ball off-balance. Regardless, I wasn't going to let him get comfortable and score without putting up a fight.

BOSTON CELTICS, December 30, 2007

L: BOSTON CELTICS, June 3, 2010. R: BOSTON CELTICS, June 6, 2010, Game Two of the NBA Finals

TONY ALLEN NEVER GOT INTIMIDATED. EVER.

He was a dog, in a good way. He was really aggressive, physical, and, most of all, he didn't quit. He was relentless. He was also old-school, in that he would foul every time and dare the refs to call it.

And . . . I loved that. I would hit him back with elbows, shove him, and reciprocate all the contact he initiated.

He's why—along with KG and them—the 2010 Finals were such a battle. They fouled me on every play and were unapologetic about it. They hit me and let me know that they hit me.

When you're in a situation like that, playing against a guy like Tony and a team like those Celtics, you have to be willing to play through that. More than that, it has to excite you on some level. You have to take it as a challenge, like, *Go ahead and be physical but trust me, you're going to back down before I do.*

RAY ALLEN WENT THROUGH A FEW DIFFERENT ON-COURT REINVENTIONS.

When he was young in Milwaukee, he just ran off of screens. Later in his stay there and in Seattle, they ran more isolations for him and let him work off of the dribble. Closer to the end, in Boston and Miami, he was back to playing entirely off of the ball and being a shooter.

Ray was deadly. He understood how to run off of screens; he understood timing; he understood how to create a tiny gap to generate the smallest windows of space. He and I had some battles, especially in his Milwaukee and Seattle days. We were in the same draft class—him, me, AI—so we were fighting to establish territory back then.

L: SEATTLE SUPERSONICS, November 24, 2005. R: MILWAUKEE BUCKS, October 24, 2002

You want to get your hips beneath those of your opponent.

That way you can alter their position by exploiting their weaker points.

I TOOK BOXING OUT A BIG MAN AS A PERSONAL CHALLENGE.

L: OKLAHOMA CITY THUNDER, December 22, 2009. R: SAN ANTONIO SPURS, February 3, 2011

In high school, we used to do these drills where you had to keep your man from getting the ball or even tapping it. If he got a hand on it, you lost the drill. So it was instilled in me that boxing out was crucial.

Outside of dominating by dint of will, there are physical ways to ensure you gain an advantage while going for a rebound. You want to, obviously, establish a good base and get your body in front of the opposition. But you also want to make sure you get lower than their hips so you can move them and alter their positioning. If you try doing that at the shoulders, it won't work because they're stronger at the top. So you want to get beneath them and use your body weight to move them from the waist down.

When most players look at basketball as a competition, they consider scoring and defending. In truth, even this little aspect—boxing out—is a competition within the competition. It's a competition to see who can get the damn ball. It's a competition to see who wants it more, and I'm not going to lose that type of battle.

L: PHILADELPHIA 76ERS, March 27, 2005. R: PHILADELPHIA 76ERS, January 6, 2006

ANDRE IGUODALA USED TO GIVE ME A LOT OF PROBLEMS.

He was really angular. More than that, his active left hand gave me problems. He had a really active left hand. You would go up to shoot, and he would just swipe the ball away from you. He does that a lot, and still pulls it off.

I had to figure out how to beat it. That was by playing mind games. Sometimes, I'd let him get the ball at first. Then have him sit on the second one, extend the ball out, and have him foul me. He'd then have to think about it. The third time, I'd hide the ball and change the angle, so there was nothing for him to swipe at. I'd play games like that, because I knew he'd never contest up high. I just had to create enough space and get him thinking about reach-ins and I'd have clean looks all day long.

L and R: SAN ANTONIO SPURS, May 21, 2008

HANDS ARE WEAPONS.

Bruce Bowen was very good at using his hands as a weapon. What he's doing here is what he would almost always do: use his left hand to hold my right arm down. Then, as I would attack, Bruce would just chop, chop, chop away at my arm to keep me from being able to cleanly dribble or pull up. It was annoying as hell, but I knew I could break free. All I had to do was ignore his arm and play through it. If I did that, which I could do because I anticipated his chops on every single play, I could beat Bruce's tactic.

ALL ABOUT FOOTWORK

When all things were equal, the best way to beat Bruce was to play through all of the bumps and chops. But if I had an angle or edge, like in this instance (in the photo above), I could just dip my shoulder and drive it right into his chest to throw his arms out of position. From there, it was all about footwork.

Look closely. My right foot is pointed in the direction I want to go—a few dribbles to the right, for a midrange jumper. If I would have wanted to cut the corner and go to the basket, I would've rotated my toes to apply more torque. In that way, footwork on-court is comparable to the way you use your head while riding a motorcycle. If you want to turn left or right, you have to start by looking and leaning your weight, starting with your head, in that direction. It's the same thing with your feet on the basketball court.

159

L: UTAH JAZZ, December 27, 2011. R: PHOENIX SUNS, February 20, 2008. Away

FIRST THINGS FIRST: SIZE UP THE DEFENSE.

In the photo at right, Shawn Marion—the help defender—is behind me. Raja Bell is trying, as you can see by his right leg, to turn me back and funnel me into Marion. That's their trap.

In turn, what I would try is using my right arm to create separation. I'd give him a slight elbow to create space, so now I could get to my pull-up jumper. Alternatively, I would drive hard at his right leg, knowing the trap was coming from the other direction, to create leverage and alter the angles enough for me to pull off a tight spin before the trap could close.

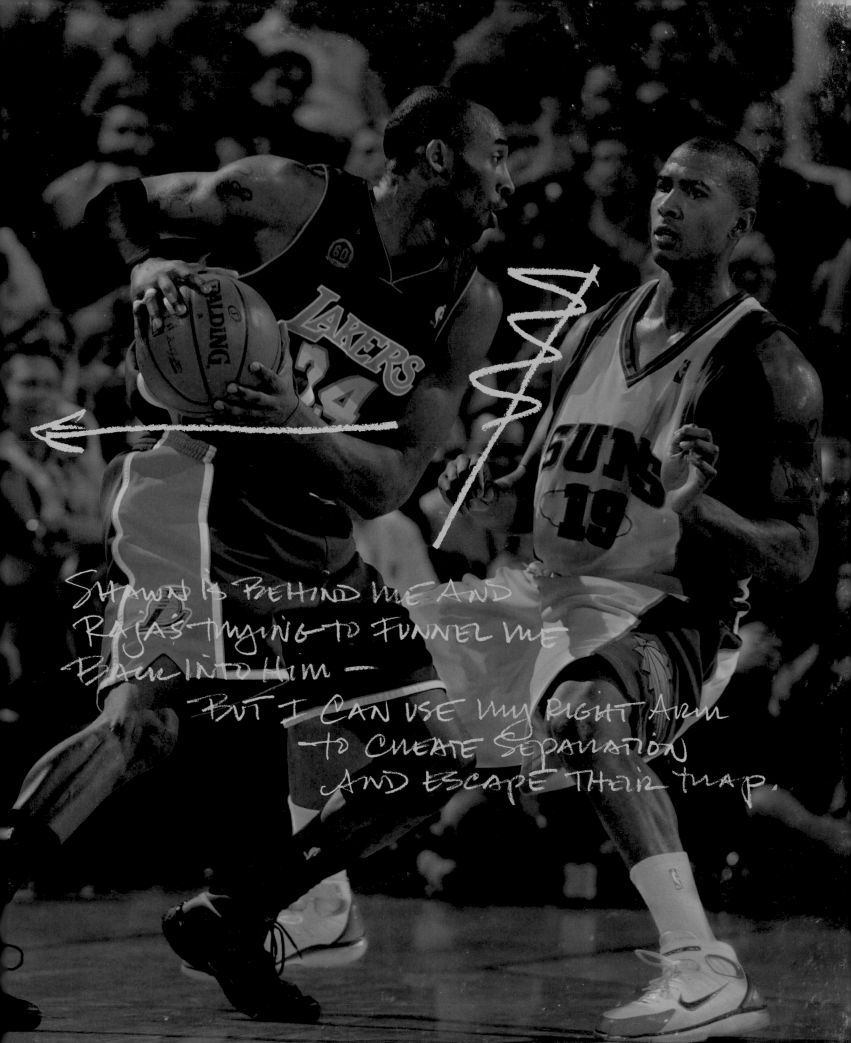

SHAWN IS BEHIND ME AND
RAJAS TRYING TO FUNNEL ME
BACK INTO HIM —
 — BUT I CAN USE MY RIGHT ARM
 — TO CREATE SEPARATION
 AND ESCAPE THEIR TRAP.

I'M SIZING UP WHERE THEY COULD THROW CARMELO THE BALL —

USING MY LEFT ARM TO DISCOURAGE THAT FROM HAPPENING.

CARMELO'S A BEAR.

I liked playing against him because he's old-school. When you hit a lot of guys repeatedly—pound, pound, pound—they'll move off the post. Not him, though. Carmelo Anthony enjoyed the physicality of it, enjoyed being hit and hitting.

Nothing was more grueling than when we matched up in the playoffs. At that point, in spite of our size difference—or maybe because of it—everything boiled down to positioning. In this instance, I'm not pushing him as much as I'm looking at the angle of the pass. I'm sizing up where they could potentially throw him the ball, and I'm using my left arm to discourage that from happening. Meanwhile, I'm using my right hand, which is out of sight, to clamp down on his arm. That way, if the pass comes, I can push his arm down, move in front, and steal the ball. Little tricks of the trade.

NEW YORK KNICKS, March 13, 2016

MY LEFT HAND KEEPS CHRIS FROM GOING TO HIS RIGHT

CAPITALIZING ON MY LENGTH SO HE STAYS BOTHERED.

CHRIS PAUL IS A SPECIAL PLAYER WHEN HE'S GOING TO HIS RIGHT SIDE.

I mean, he's good going left, too—but he's tremendous going to his right. Obviously then, my first line of defense is tying up his right hand. As you can see, I would put my left hand there to let him know that if you try going right, I'm going to take the ball from you or, at least, make it hard for you to pick up the ball.

Also, I would use my height and length advantage to bother him. When he would go up to shoot, I would contest. When he would go to drive, I would body him. When he would go to pass, I'd try to read the angles and cut them off by using my length. Anything, really, to throw him off his game.

Another method I employed was anticipation. The best way to anticipate what CP—what anyone—is going to do is by studying their game. If you do that, you'll know what they like to do in certain places, and you can predict that and become the aggressor.

CHRIS DEFENDED WITH CRAFT.

He was quick, strong, and supremely intelligent.

If I had position on him in the post, he'd try to cheat to one side to play the passing lane. That way, if it was an errant pass, he'd be able to poke the ball loose or steal it outright. My reaction to that was to use my size to keep him behind me, so he couldn't lean in either direction, and catch the ball up high. Then, when I turned to shoot the fadeaway over him, I would hold the ball high and never bring it down to his level. That's something I worked on a lot in the summer—catching the ball, turning, and keeping the ball in front of my face.

DWYANE WADE WOULD JUST VANISH.

There was no one harder to guard off a screen-roll than Dwyane. That's a sweeping but true statement, and a lot factored into his skill. Mainly, he had such a strong base, and could get so low to the ground, that once he came off of the screen he was gone. He would just vanish. It was really, really hard for me—and for our big men, who he would split and leave in the dust—to guard him.

Ultimately, I had to sit down and watch a lot of film with our bigs. I showed them that I needed them to hold him up for one second, then I could get back to him. Now, a second might not sound like a lot of time, but he was blowing by guys in .2 seconds. So, I really had to drill that into our bigs.

The first year or two, yeah, I could sag off of Dwyane a little bit and buy that extra time and space. By his third year, nah. Even though his shot didn't look good, it went in, so you had to respect it. His shot only got better and more fluid from there.

L: MIAMI HEAT, December 25, 2006, Away. R: MIAMI HEAT, February 28, 2008

A YOUNG KEVIN DURANT WASN'T THAT DIFFICULT TO HANDLE.

During his first few years in the NBA, KD had certain deficiencies in his game that I would exploit. At the time, he struggled shooting pull-up jumpers while going to his right side and he didn't know how to operate in the post. Those holes, despite his immense height, made him guardable. Fairly quickly though—within a year or two—he became proficient at pulling up on his right side. A few years after that, he added a few left-shoulder post moves. Before I knew it, he was a 7-foot handful on the court.

And that's Kevin Durant's story.

For almost a decade, he did nothing but address weaknesses and add to his game. Now, his skill set is completely fleshed out. His offensive game has no weaknesses. He's a nightmare to go up against, and he's worked to achieve that status.

THE TALENT HAS ALWAYS BEEN THERE FOR JAMES HARDEN.

Even though he was coming off the bench, James was the reason we lost the series to the Thunder in 2011. Russell and KD in the starting five, we could deal with those guys. But then you go to the bench and James was just coming in. We didn't have anyone who could match up with him. In the fourth quarter, when they all played at the same time, we were always at a disadvantage. He was the key to that team.

James always had an innate ability to read pick-and-roll situations. He could get into the paint and draw fouls. He could shoot. He could use his mass to bully lighter guards. Ultimately, I don't think Oklahoma realized exactly what they had. I knew, but I don't think they did.

L: OKLAHOMA CITY THUNDER, May 16, 2012, 2012, Away. R: HOUSTON ROCKETS, April 10, 2016, Away

WHEN I GOT HURT, I NEVER DWELLED ON WHAT HAPPENED.

Over the course of 20 seasons, I suffered my fair share of serious injuries. The first thing I always thought about in those situations was, "What do I need to do to get back to 100 percent?" That was my mindset. I never let fear or doubt seep into my psyche. I never whined and I never complained. I mean, for what?

On the fractures, small breaks, and sprains I asked myself a different question: "Will it get worse if I play through it?" If it was going to be painful but not get worse, I'd deal with it 100 percent of the time. That was the only thought process for me.

I fought through some injuries—ankles, back, knees, shoulders—that limited me in certain ways. In those instances, I'd spend time during shootaround and early in the game testing out what I could and couldn't do on the court. Once I established my limitations, I'd adjust my gameplan accordingly. Occasions like that are reminders why you need to have a well-rounded game, why you need to be able to do everything with both hands, off of either foot, whether you're 30 feet from the basket or in the post.

When I was hurt, I was less athletic. It limited some of my burst and explosion. But that's all it did. I was still me, still Kobe.

ORLANDO MAGIC, June 14, 2009, Away

EMOTIONS ARE A MAJOR
COMPONENT OF BASKETBALL.

The game is full of ebbs and flows—the good, the bad, and everything in between. With all that was going on around me, I had to figure out how to steel my mind and keep calm and centered. That's not to say my emotions didn't spike or drop here or there, but I was aware enough to recalibrate and bring them back level before things spiraled. I could do that in a way others couldn't, and that was really key for me.

I ENJOYED CONTACT.

LeBron is bigger than me in height and width, but I enjoyed hitting, and getting hit, a lot more than him. That impacted our head-to-head matchups.

When he was defending me, LeBron would use his body and not cushion with his forearm because he was used to being stronger than everybody else. With me, though, that worked to my advantage. I like the physicality, and I know how to use my hands to move him back just enough where I could turn the corner. Then, the next time down the court he would have to overcompensate for that and I could spin baseline for a shot or drive.

At a certain point, he started fronting me in the post. I would come down and tease him. "I'm 6-5, why are you fronting me in the post?" He would say, "Nope, I'm not falling for that. I don't want you catching it down here."

Over time, I saw him mature greatly as a defensive player. He understood the significance and importance of it. He understood that if you want to win a championship, you, the star, have to take on the responsibility of guarding the other team's best player. I always prided myself on guarding the best.

LEBRON WOULDN'T CUSHION WITH HIS FOREARM—

BUT I LIKE THE PHYSICALITY AND USE MY ARM TO MOVE HIM BACK.

THIS IS PRETTY SIMPLE.

For these types of traps, I had to stay alive as a threat. If I could do that, I could manipulate the defense and dictate the action.

What does that look like? I would attack these two defenders and suck them down towards the corner. Then, there were gaps on the weak side of the floor for my teammates to occupy. In most cases, I would end up with the assist or the hockey assist after rotating the ball the other way. Alternatively, I could slow down my pacing and draw Channing Frye towards me. Then, I'd have the angle and I would drive right around him for two.

When it came to making the pass, it never mattered which four teammates were on the court with me. If I allowed that to factor into my decision making, the defense would have the upper hand. Instead, through preparation and film study, I was able to tell my teammates in the morning during shootaround where to be during that night's game. I was able to tell them when they see the defense do X, they should do Y; when they see Y, do Z. In that way, we—as a unit—were always able to own the defense.

CLEVELAND CAVALIERS, March 10, 2016

RUSSELL CHERISHED THE CHALLENGE OF TRYING TO STOP ME.

In turn, I loved showing him my full arsenal of weapons. One of them was mental: knowing my opponent. I knew he was competitive, as much then as he is now, so I knew he would bite at the opportunity to block my shot. So I'd throw him a hard pump fake and either get fouled or go right by him.

That was just Russ being youthful. He had to learn, and I was there to teach him.

As time progressed, I'd attack him with a little bit of everything. The goal, though, was to shoot over the top—I had a few inches on him—and take him to spots on the floor where I could overpower him. I didn't want to dribble or fuss with the ball when he was on me. I'd slice to the post, move to the elbow, and be patient.

L: OKLAHOMA CITY THUNDER, May 19, 2012. R: OKLAHOMA CITY THUNDER, January 8, 2016

WHEN RUSS CAME INTO THE LEAGUE, HE WAS A DIFFERENT PLAYER.

At first, Russ couldn't really shoot. That made it easy to corral him. I knew where he wanted to go with the ball and could cut off his angles. As his jumper became more consistent, he became more of a problem. At that point, I would try to frustrate him as much as possible. I would pick at him. Arms, elbows, little grabs here, holds there. Here, I'm locking up his right arm off of the dribble. If he picks up the ball, I'm going to yank at his arm a little bit but enough for him to feel it. Tricks of the trade that the ref can't see. Then, his battle would be with the officials instead of with me.

Also, when he was young, Russell was really streaky. I used to play off of him, make him think it was a good idea to take shots against me. Later, when he started hitting them consistently, he forced me to mix it up. At that point, I really had to contemplate how best to guard him. I'd try to disrupt his rhythm. For instance, when he was barreling down the court, contemplating pulling up for a jumper, I'd feign a jab at him. That would change his mind and make him think he could drive all the way to the basket, except I could then back up and take away his rhythm.

It was hard, though, especially when he was coming at full speed. Like LeBron, when Russ got a head of steam it was a problem, so I had to jam him up as soon as our team shot the ball. It really became a fun game of cat-and-mouse.

Russell continues to evolve; he is a constant learner. This past year, when he was 29, he came to Orange County, and we would work out for a few hours at 5 AM. At that age, most guys in the league think they know it all. He wanted to work on his post game, on footwork in the post. He realized that was the next step in his evolution and the key to his longevity.

That's the money right there, that thirst and quest for information and improvement. So, we spent quite a bit of time working on that, and I saw him use some of the lessons we worked on in game action as soon as the season started.

L: NBA Championship Ring Ceremony, October 26, 2010. R: Training camp, September 27, 2010

DEREK WAS A NATURAL LEADER.

Some people are born leaders; some people become leaders. Derek Fisher, no doubt, was born with that skill. From the day he reported to L.A. out of Little Rock, he was a stable influence and guiding force—albeit a soothing one—for the Lakers.

I think some of his leadership was natural; a lot of it was also nurture. It was, seemingly, infused into him by his family, his upbringing in Arkansas, and the route he took to get to the highest level.

Regardless of the source of his preternatural leadership powers, I would go to battle with Derek.

Derek constantly worked on his game. One of the aspects he improved significantly over the years was his jump shot. When Derek came into the league, he was just OK from the field. He realized pretty quickly that he would need to retool his J. So he worked relentlessly at it and became not just a good shooter but a dead-eye.

Derek was really good with the ball. He protected the rock like a point guard should, and rarely turned it over. He also made solid decisions.

As far as his role on the team went, though, he was always more valuable than just the sum of his game. He was always patient, and we offset each other quite a bit. That's part of what made us such a lethal combo.

THE BASKET STAYS STATIONARY.

When someone like Shane Battier face-guarded me it didn't really impact my game. I believed that I could just shoot through it. The basket wasn't moving, so muscle memory just kicked into work. I didn't have to see the rim to make a bucket.

Shane, as a whole, was a solid defensive player. He was smart, too, smart enough to understand that talking trash riled me up. Shane, as a counter to that, would tell people he couldn't guard me. By doing that, Shane thought he was going to take the bite out of my game, take the edge off. But I saw through that tactic, understood his premeditated modesty, and attacked him because of it. Safe to say, I had a lot of fun playing against him.

L: MIAMI HEAT, January 17, 2013. R: HOUSTON ROCKETS, May 10, 2009, Away

METTA REALIZED OUR TEAM WAS DIFFERENT.

Soon after he joined the Lakers, Metta World Peace came to the gym one day and found me working out. He was surprised to see me there. I said to him, "How do you think we get these championships?" Metta responded by talking about how much talent we had on the roster. I cut him off, and told him, "Metta, winning rings isn't easy. If you think because you're here, because we have Pau and Lamar, that this is already a done deal? You and I are going to have problems."

I let him know that I didn't care what he did and what he got into off the court, but when he was at practice, when he was in the gym, I needed him to be present mentally. I needed him there ready to compete in every drill, to work every second, and to win every scrimmage. He showed up every day and worked his tail off. We never had any issue.

Metta is one of the smartest defensive players I ever suited up with. He was fundamentally sound, and had a sturdy frame, quick hands, and quick feet. Above all, he was tenacious. When he was on defense, he was like a dog with a bone—he just wouldn't let go.

Metta's goal was to guard someone and take them completely out of the game. He wanted to fluster and intimidate them. He and I would have a good time with that. We would talk before games about who we were going to shut down and punk that night. We'd be like, "You take him the first five possessions, I'll take the next five, and then we'll trap him and beat him down."

Yeah, I loved playing with Metta. He was able to deal with, and even sought out, tough love. He wanted me to let him know, "Look, enough of that. We're going to win a championship, so don't mess it up." Most people wouldn't do that with him. They were either intimidated or scared by how he might respond. He knew I wasn't, and he respected that.

DOUBLED DOWN

I would—this is no secret—take the ball to the basket. That's just what I would do. I relished the challenge, the contact, the decision making. In response, opponents would prepare for my hard takes by collapsing and swarming me with two, three, four defenders.

When they did that, it was a wrap for them because I was in control. I was in control of the action and the whole flow of the game. I was in control of whether I would finish strong or pivot back around and find open shooters on the perimeter. A large part of that in-air decision was based on scouting individual and team tendencies. I would know who would jump vertically and allow me to finish. Likewise, I would know who was more confrontational and likely to foul me or leave an open passing lane. It all depended on who was waiting for me at the basket and what the smart play was going to be.

L: HOUSTON ROCKETS, October 30, 2007. R: GOLDEN STATE WARRIORS, November 15, 2002

DEEPER THAN HOOPS

Pau Gasol was like a brother to me. Over the course of my career, I suited up with dozens upon dozens of players. Among all of them, it's safe to say that Pau was my favorite teammate ever.

We traded for Pau in the middle of the 2008 season, and he and I connected immediately. I remember going to his hotel room, pretty much as soon as he settled in, and we talked and got to know each other. I could feel the bond forming instantly, and it lasts to this day.

He was a very intelligent player, very detail-oriented. More than that, he had a big heart and just as big a drive to win. That was a common language that we spoke. The other common language was Spanish, and I think that played a part in our fast friendship. In general, we were both very culturally diverse. We both loved reading and musicals and opera and theater. We had a connection that ran deeper than hoops.

L: ORLANDO MAGIC, June 3, 2009. Away. R: NEW YORK KNICKS, December 25, 2012

WINNING CHAMPIONSHIPS IS EVERYTHING.

It's really one of the greatest joys on this planet. That feeling drove me to always want more. When I won one ring, I wanted two. When I won two, I wanted three.

I think that drive stemmed from being part of a rebuilding process, after struggling for a few years and working and working to reach that pinnacle. Once I reached it, I wanted to achieve more. I never wanted to experience the still-familiar feeling of defeat again.

THE AGONY OF DEFEAT IS AS LOW AS
THE JOY OF WINNING IS HIGH.

I BUILT MY GAME TO HAVE NO HOLES.

It doesn't matter how well you knew my game. It doesn't matter if we played against each other for years, or were even teammates for a stretch. None of that helped you guard me.

Yes, you might have known I preferred to go one way. That didn't ultimately matter, because I could just as easily go the other way. Yeah, you might have also thought you knew my cadence and rhythm, except—I didn't have one. I made a point to adjust the pace of my attack to throw defenders off. In essence, the more you thought you knew about my game, the harder it would actually be to guard me.

You can pick up a nuance or weakness by studying tape and paying attention during workouts. In fact, I was constantly scouting teammates and opponents. I would learn how physically complete their game was, how perse-verant they were, and identify weaknesses right there and then. I would file that away until we eventually played against each other.

I did this in the off-season too, and during my stint with Team USA. Particularly, I used to relentlessly tease LeBron and KD about their lack of skills in the post. To their credit, however, they developed that part of their game and now can operate comfortably down there.

What separates great players from all-time great players is their ability to self-assess, diagnose weaknesses, and turn those flaws into strengths.

I LOST TRACK OF TIME.

I started the final day of my NBA career at the office. I was working on some stories and exciting future projects and just got wrapped up in the work. Next thing I knew, I looked up and realized it was already time to go.

The trip to Staples Center was just another trip for me. It might have been the 1,346th and final regular season game for me, but it felt like any other. The mood at the arena didn't feel that way, though. When I arrived, there was a palpable, somber energy. It felt sort of sad, and I didn't want that. I wanted the night to be a celebration; I wanted the night to be full of life, and I realized it was on me to change the vibes.

After I suited up and hit the court, I could tell I didn't have my legs. In that moment I realized: It was going to be one of the greatest performances of all time or one of the worst. I kind of laughed at that thought for a second, smiled because I always stayed prepared to play on leaden legs; then I just went out and hooped.

The game started and I was acutely focused. I was in the moment, and any small thoughts of it being the final game disappeared. The game became *the* game—the game I played professionally nearly every day for 20 years. The tactical game that I excelled in. The game of chess that I always played and loved.

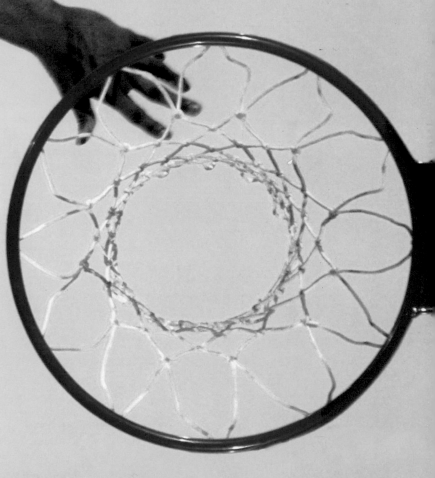

BASKETBALL TOOK ME EVERYWHERE.

The game provided me with every opportunity that I ever imagined it would, and along the way I learned a innumerable amount. I'm not just speaking about on the court, either. Without hoops, I would not understand how to create or write, I would not understand human nature, nor would I know how to lead.

The game, in essence, taught me the art of storytelling. Without it, I would not have an Emmy, I would not have an Oscar, I would not have creative dreams and visions still to unfold.

Yeah, basketball took me everywhere. Now, I'm taking the game everywhere.

C. 1999, Great Western Forum, Inglewood, California

33,643

CAREER REGULAR-SEASON POINTS

Third-most all-time behind Kareem Abdul-Jabbar and Karl Malone. Only three other players totaled 25,000 points, 6,000 rebounds, and 6,000 assists in their careers: Oscar Robertson, John Havlicek, and LeBron James.

81

POINTS
The second-most points ever scored in an NBA game and the most since the three-point line was introduced to the league in 1979.

37

YEARS OLD
Kobe's age when he scored 60 points in his final NBA game, the most by any player in the 2015-16 season.

20

SEASONS
Devoted to the Lakers, the longest tenure by any guard with one team in NBA history.

18

YEARS OLD
Whe Kobe made his first NBA start.

When Kobe became the youngest player to win the NBA Slam Dunk contest.

When Kobe became the youngest player ever to score in a playoff game.

5

CHAMPIONSHIPS
Won, including the three-peat of 2000, 2001, and 2002, followed by 2009 and 2010.

2

JERSEY NUMBERS
Retired in Los Angeles: 8 and 24.

FINALS MVP AWARDS

SCORING TITLES
In consecutive years.

OLYMPIC GOLD MEDALS
In two attempts.

CHRONOLOGY

JUNE 26, 1996
Bryant is selected 13th overall in the NBA draft by the Charlotte Hornets. As part of a pre-agreed deal his rights are traded to the Los Angeles Lakers five days later.

NOVEMBER 3, 1996
At 18 years and 72 days, Bryant becomes at the time the youngest player ever to play in an NBA game.

FEBRUARY 8, 1998
Voted in by fans, Bryant becomes the youngest All-Star in league history and scores a team-high 18 points for the Western Conference.

JUNE 14, 2000
Returning from an ankle injury suffered in Game 2 of the Finals, Kobe hits three clutch shots in Game 4, including the go-ahead putback layup to seal an overtime win over the Pacers and a 3–1 series lead. Bryant wins his first championship five days later.

2001
The Lakers beat the Philadelphia 76ers in five games for a second straight title.

2002
L.A. returns to the Finals and completes a three-peat with a clean sweep of the New Jersey Nets.

FEBRUARY 2003
Bryant averages 40.6 points per game for the month of February.

2004
The Lakers return to the Finals for the fourth time in five years, but fall to the Pistons in five games.

JANUARY 22, 2006
Bryant scores a career-high 81 points in a win over the Toronto Raptors.

2008
Bryant is named league MVP after leading the Lakers to the best record in the West, battling through a serious finger injury in his shooting hand. He becomes the Lakers' all-time leading scorer in the process. The Lakers fall to the Celtics in the Finals in six games.

JUNE 2008
Bryant and Team USA's "Redeem Team" secure a gold medal in Beijing.

2009
The Lakers roll to another NBA championship in five games against the Orlando Magic. Bryant is named Finals MVP.

2010
At the end of an epic series, Bryant pockets his fifth championship and second Finals MVP award, getting revenge over the Celtics and helping the Lakers back from a 13-point second-half deficit in Game 7 to seal the title.

APRIL 12, 2013
Bryant tears his Achilles tendon in a game against the Warriors.

DECEMBER 14, 2014
Bryant takes his place as the NBA's third all-time leading scorer, surpassing Michael Jordan's 32,292-point mark.

NOVEMBER 29, 2015
Kobe announces his forthcoming retirement at the end of the season.

APRIL 13, 2016
In the final game of his career, Bryant scores a remarkable 60 points on the road in Utah, including 23 fourth-quarter points to ice a five-point win over the Jazz.

1996

2000

On the court with Shaquille O'Neal, during Game 2 of the Finals, in which Kobe badly sprained his ankle.

2001

2010

L: Going to the basket against the Boston Celtics in Game 2 of the Finals.
R: Presenting a jersey to President Barack Obama, along with Derek Fisher, at the White House.

2008

2013

Moments after tearing his Achilles tendon, in a game against the Golden State Warriors at Staples Center.

2016

I HAD NEVER HEARD STAPLES CENTER GO SO QUIET AS IT DID WHEN KOBE WENT DOWN.

He was holding his Achilles, pulling at the tendon that was no longer there, trying to reattach it. It was like Achilles himself had fallen, cut down in his prime, grasping at a career that might never rebound. But if anyone could come back from such a serious injury, it was Kobe. It had to be Kobe. His determination and focus were superhuman; his commitment to the game was nothing short of devout. What else could explain a player who scores 60 points in his final game?

I took Kobe's rookie headshot (shown on page 205) in October of 1996. The fresh-faced, 18-year-old rookie was a ball of energy. But he held an intense curiosity. Kobe observed everyone and everything. And for his age, he was uncharacteristically focused and motivated. I was 38, and a new father of two, and I was about to watch this young man who so many were calling the next Michael Jordan become the one and only Kobe Bryant.

Those three championships that Kobe won with Shaq were historic: men against boys, playing an entirely different game. In that era, the Lakers were invincible. And it was in the whirlwind of glory—but in setbacks, too—that Kobe became a man.

That hothead rookie of '96 had been a fierce competitor, even at practice. He couldn't lose. And as his career unfolded, Kobe would take his relentless pursuit of perfection—that academic obsession—and mold it into his unique personality as a leader. Kobe was always vocal in the locker room and training room. But he also knew how to escape to that quiet place and mentally prepare for the game ahead. By the time he had been branded an elder statesman on Team USA and in All-Star Games, Kobe was a serial winner who could fire up his teammates and steel himself like a warrior monk.

But few people have seen another side to Kobe: the man who performed Make-A-Wish requests after almost every home game—and many road games—throughout his career. I got to document a few of those nights when Kobe was there for kids and their families as a different kind of hero— one who understood the profound impact of basketball beyond simply winning and losing. Behind Kobe's relentless determination was a gentle and sober compassion.

There are only a few NBA players who were consistently dynamic and exciting to photograph, game after game, year after year. A very short list: Magic, MJ, and Kobe. Early in his career Kobe was a dunk machine. I remember my disappointment when I didn't come home with three or four dunk photos after a game. That eagerness for the big, exciting shot abated as the years went by. Kobe continued to be an amazing subject to photograph on the court, but the fun was in the challenge of documenting the intensity and passion, the subtlety and detail that came out in his game; those epic matchups that really got his juices flowing.

Off the court I was fortunate to forge a great relationship with Kobe rooted in mutual respect and trust. Twenty years is a long time in life—and especially in basketball— to be a fly on the wall. But Kobe knew I had a job to do, and I knew how to respect his privacy and his space. The result is an unparalleled insight into the career of a legend. As Kobe steps away from the court, he returns to his fans transformed: Now he has become a teacher, reflecting on the game he changed and sharing his hard-won wisdom.

—**ANDREW D. BERNSTEIN**

INDEX

ANDREW D. BERNSTEIN's photography has appeared in thousands of newspapers and on magazine covers worldwide. Bernstein is the long-time official photographer for the Los Angeles Lakers and the senior photographer for the NBA. He is the 2018 recipient of the Curt Gowdy Media Award from the Naismith Memorial Basketball Hall of Fame. He regularly appears on ESPN's *SportsCenter* and other national television and radio programs.

KOBE BRYANT is one of the most accomplished and celebrated athletes of all time. Over the course of his twenty-year career—all played with the Los Angeles Lakers—he won five NBA championships, two Olympic gold medals, eighteen All-Star selections, and four All-Star Game MVP awards, among many other achievements. Bryant retired in 2016. He lives in Southern California with his wife, Vanessa, and their three daughters. He still claims he's never been beaten one on one.